Anne Frank

The Truth About Anne Frank's Life Revealed

(Anne Frank Beyond Her Diary Includes the Lost Anne Frank Video)

Carlos Pantoja

Published By **Tyson Maxwell**

Carlos Pantoja

All Rights Reserved

Anne Frank: The Truth About Anne Frank's Life Revealed (Anne Frank Beyond Her Diary Includes the Lost Anne Frank Video)

ISBN 978-1-77485-744-1

No part of this guidebook shall be reproduced in any form without permission in writing from the publisher except in the case of brief quotations embodied in critical articles or reviews.

Legal & Disclaimer

The information contained in this ebook is not designed to replace or take the place of any form of medicine or professional medical advice. The information in this ebook has been provided for educational & entertainment purposes only.

The information contained in this book has been compiled from sources deemed reliable, and it is accurate to the best of the Author's knowledge; however, the Author cannot guarantee its accuracy and validity and cannot be held liable for any errors or omissions. Changes are periodically made to this book. You must consult your doctor or get professional medical advice before using any of the suggested remedies, techniques, or information in this book.

Upon using the information contained in this book, you agree to hold harmless the Author from and against any damages, costs, and expenses, including any legal fees potentially resulting from the application of any of the information provided by this guide. This disclaimer applies to any damages or injury caused by the use and application, whether directly or indirectly, of any advice or information presented, whether for breach of contract, tort, negligence, personal injury, criminal intent, or under any other cause of action.

You agree to accept all risks of using the information presented inside this book. You need to consult a professional medical practitioner in order to ensure you are both able and healthy enough to participate in this program.

TABLE OF CONTENTS

Chapter 1: Who Was Anne Frank? 1

Chapter 2: Her Youngness Prior To The Diary 5

Chapter 3: Time Of Her Diary 11

Chapter 4: Apprehended And Deported And Then Executed 22

Chapter 5 The Diary's Publication 37

Chapter 6: The Early Years 51

Chapter 7: A Storm Is Brewing 66

Chapter 8: What She Did? 77

Conclusion 184

Chapter 1: Who Was Anne Frank?

Annelies Marie Frank was a Jewish diarist from Germany who was Dutch-German. Her popularity grew following the publication of The Diary of a Girl (previously Het Achterhuis in Dutch; English: The Secret Annex) The Diary of a Girl, in which she outlines her experiences in the shadows during the German occupation in the Netherlands during The Second World War. It's among the most popular books around the world, and has been the inspiration for countless films and plays.

Born in Frankfurt, Germany, and was a frequent visitor to or around Amsterdam, Netherlands, having actually relocated to the city with her family after Adolf Hitler and the Nazi Party assumed the control over Germany in 1934, at four and a half years old.

Learn about the young woman who was famous following her death and wrote her thoughts in a journal while being hidden in the Nazi army, who were hunting Jews in World War II.

Her birthplace was in Germany but was denied citizenship in 1941, making her without a state. The German control of the Netherlands was a restriction on to the Franks in Amsterdam in May 1940. When the Franks were in Amsterdam, July 1942 was as the persecution of Jews was intensified, they sought refuge in the secluded areas behind a bookcase within the building where her father, Otto Frank, worked. Anne kept a journal she received for her birthday and would write in it regularly throughout the time until her family's detention by the Gestapo during the month of August 1944. The Franks were taken to detention centers following their arrest. Anne as well as her younger sister Margot was transferred out of Auschwitz and transferred to Bergen-Belsen the death camp, on the 1st of November in 1944. They died a couple of months afterward (potentially from typhus). It was reported that the Red Cross had formerly computed that they died in March in addition, Dutch authorities had deemed the 31st of March as their primary date of death. According to The Diary of Anne Frank the Critical Edition, released in 1986, researchers David Barnouw and Gerrald van der Stroom suggested that they died at the end of February or beginning of March 1945. This was according to the written testimony of an eyewitness Lien Brilleslijper, who was in November 1945. Based on research conducted by the Anne Frank Home in 2015, they were dead in February.

Following the conflict, Otto, the Frank family's sole survivor went home to Amsterdam to discover that his assistant, Miep Gies, had kept Anne's diary. In 1947, he made the decision to grasp Anne's dream of as an author by publishing her diaries. It was released as an English in the form of The Diary of a Girl in 1952 after it was translated from the original Dutch edition. It was then transliterated into more than seventy languages.

Chapter 2: Her Youngness Prior To The Diary

Edith (nee Hollander) and Otto Heinrich Frank brought to life Annelies or Anneliese Marie Frank on June 12th in the year 1929, at the Maingau Red Cross Center in Frankfurt, Germany. Margot Frank, her elder sibling, was the sole sibling or brother. Franks were a family of Franks are liberal Jews who didn't adhere to the rules of Judaism and traditions. They lived civilisation comprised of Jews and non-Jews with diverse religions. Edith as well as Otto were happy grandparents or parents who enjoyed taking part in school-related activities and an enormous library. Both parents pushed their children to read.

The family was renting 2 floors in a house located in Marbachweg 307, in Frankfurt-Dornbusch at the time of the birth of Anne. In 1931, they relocated into Ganghoferstrasse 24, which was located within Dornbusch's Dichterviertel (Poets Quarter) which was a fashionable open region. Both houses are still in use.

Edith Frank and her kids moved to stay with Edith's mother Rosa in Aachen following the time that Adolf Hitler's Nazi Party won the federal election. Hitler was elected to be the new Chancellor of the Reich. Otto Frank remained in Frankfurt however, when he was given the opportunity to start a business in Amsterdam and he moved there to run the company and to find a home that would accommodate his entire family. He was employed by his employer, the Opekta Works, a business that offered pectin, which is an extract from fruit. Edith moved from Aachen and Amsterdam in search of an apartment, or condominium in the Merwedeplein (Merwede Square) in Amsterdam's Rivierenbuurt neighborhood that was home to numerous Jewish-German refugees. Edith took her husband with her to Amsterdam in November 1933. Margot joined her a month after. Anne lived with her mother until the family returned to Amsterdam during February. Between 1933-1939 over 300,000 Jews were evicted from Germany including the Franks.

Anne as well as Margot Frank were both enrolled in school after they moved from Amsterdam, Margot in public school and Anne in the sixth Montessori School. Despite having initial difficulties dealing with Dutch tongue, Margot rose to the highest at her school in Amsterdam. Anne quickly felt at home within the Montessori classroom where she was able to meet kids who were her age and this included Hanneli Goslar who would eventually become one of her best acquaintances.

In 1938 Otto Frank established Pectacon which was a wholesaler of marinading salts, herbs and mixed spices utilized for the making of sausages.

Pectacon employs Hermann van Pels as a spice consultant. He was a former resident of Osnabruck along with his parents in the year 1939 to become an Jewish butcher. Edith Frank's mother moved in the Franks in 1939. She stayed with them until she died in January 1942.

When Germany began to attack the Netherlands in May, 1940 the professional federal government began to discriminate against Jews by enacting restrictive and unjust laws, and additionally, required registration and division.

Otto Frank tried to schedule the family's move into in the United States, which he considered to be the only viable alternative . However, his visa application wasn't ever considered due to issues such as the closing of the USA consulate in Rotterdam and the destruction to all documentation, which also included an application for visa. Even if the application had been completed and approved, it was believed that the U.S.A. authorities was scared that family members who remained in Germany might be scared into being Nazi spy agencies.

Anne was aware during the summer holiday season in 1941 that she was not be permitted to attend the Montessori School just because Jewish students had to be within Jewish schools. Anne as did her sister Margot was the first to join the Jewish Lyceum after that.

Chapter 3: Time Of Her Diary

Frank received a special book that was bound in red and white checkered fabric that had a small lock at the front for Frank's 13th birthday. Frank took it to use to keep a journal, and began writing in it almost immediately. She discusses a variety of restrictions placed on the life that were imposed on those in the Dutch Jewish population in her journal, which was published on June 20 in 1942.

The systematic removal of Jews from the Netherlands began in the summer of 1942.

Margot received a phone call from the Zentralstelle for Judische Auswanderung (Headquarters for Jewish Emigration) on July 5th, 1942, directing her to report to a camp for laborers and requesting Otto as well as Edith Frank to move the plan forward by 10 days. Anne handed over a book tea set, as well as the tin filled with marbles to her close neighbour and neighbor next door Toosje Kupers before escaping to hiding. Kupers's family Frank family wrote a note to Kupers on July 6th. Kupers on the 6th of July asking the Kupers to look after Moortje, their pet. Moortje. As per The Associated Press: "' I'm not happy with my marbles due to the fact that I'm scary. They could end up in wrong hands" Anne stated to Kupers. "Could you perhaps keep them for me? '".

The Frank family relocated to their hideout which was a three-story building that was accessed from an elevated landing over the Opekta workplaces located on the Prinsengracht in Amsterdam, which was where some of Otto's most trusted workers would become their assistants. This was in the early morning of July 6th, Monday 1942. They called it the Achterhuis is the title that was given to this place of refuge (translated to "Secret Annexe" in English versions of his diary). Their house was disorganized to convey an impression that they'd gone on a sudden leave in addition, Otto wrote a letter indicating that they had left for Switzerland. They had to take Anne's cats, Moortje in the house as due to the necessity to hide. Otto, Edith, and Anne went a distance of a few miles from their homes because Jews weren't allowed to take advantage of public transport. Miep Gies as well as Margot rode bicycles up to Prinsengracht. To ensure that the Achterhuis was not visible it was covered with the bookcase.

The only employees who knew of the individuals who were hiding included Victor Kugler, Johannes Kleiman, Miep

Gies, and Bep Voskuijl. They were "assistants" throughout the duration of their confinement, together as were Gies his wife Jan Gies and Voskuijl's dad Johannes Hendrik Voskuijl. They were the sole connection with the rest of the world as well as the residents, keeping them informed of news about war and political events. They met all their needs, ensured their safety, and supplied their families with food, an endeavor that became more difficult as the years progressed. Frank spoke about their dedication and effort to keep home in a positive mood throughout the most difficult of times. They all knew that if they got caught and convicted, they could be imprisoned for concealing Jews.

Van Pels comprising Hermann, Auguste, and 16-year-old Peter joined the Franks on July 13th in 1942. as well Fritz Pfeffer, a dental specialist and family member who joined them in November. Frank expressed her delight at getting to know new people, however tension quickly developed among the group who were forced to live in such cramped living spaces. She considered Pfeffer irritating and resentful of his presence after sharing a space with him. In addition, she had a heated argument over Auguste van Pels, whom she considered to be a joke. Hermann van Pels and Fritz Pfeffer were, according to her, were selfish, especially in relation at the volume of food they ate. After ignoring the awkward and shy Peter van Pels initially, she fell in love with him , and the two began dating. She was able to kiss him once for the very first time however, her affection for him waned as she wondered whether her feelings for him was genuine or the effect of their imprisonment together. Every volunteer formed an intimate relationship to Anne Frank, and Otto Frank later remarked that she awaited their daily visits with great apprehension. Anne's most trusted close friend was Bep Voskuijl "the younger typing machine ... The two of them would often be silent at the corners," according to him.

Frank focused on her relationships with the members of the family and the subtle differences in their personalities, in her writing. Frank believed that she was the closest in terms of mental proximity to her father and later stated, "Anne and I got much better along than Margot and was closer to her mother. It's possible that this was due to the fact that Margot never expressed her thoughts and didn't require more help than Anne did since she wasn't as prone to mood fluctuations." While

Anne occasionally displayed jealousy towards Margot particularly when family members ridiculed Anne for her lack of Margot's calm, serene character The Frank sisters shared a more intimate relationship than they did before going into hiding. They were able to talk to each other in the course of Anne became older. Frank observed on January 12, 1944 that in her journalthat "Margot is much more friendly ... It's clear that she's not as rude anymore and is turning into an extremely good friend. She doesn't see me as to be a child who doesn't have any significance."

Frank often wrote about her strained relationship to her mother and her mixed feelings about her. "She's not a mother to me." Frank wrote on the 7th in 1942, when she outlined her "contempt" for her mother and her reluctance to "face her in the face of her insanity, her sarcasm and her sarcasm." Frank found herself resentful of her irrational attitude later when she altered her diary entry, adding: "Anne, is it really you who spoke of hatred in the first place? Oh Anne and how did you manage to do it?" Frank realized that their arguments stemmed from faulty beliefs, which were similar to her and her mom's faults. She also realized she had unintentionally contributed to the suffering of her mother. Frank began treating her mom with more understanding and respect following this realization.

All member of the Frank sisters was preparing for their return to school as soon as they could and went on to study in secret. Margot completed a correspondence class with 'Elementary Latin' Bep Voskuijl's honor and received excellent marks. Anne spent the majority of her time studying and reading as she wrote and altered daily diary entries (after the month of March, 1944). She also wrote about her feelings, beliefs aspirations, dreams and hopes concerns she believed she was unable to discuss with anyone else and also told the details of the events taking place. She wrote about more abstract topics such as her belief in God and her understanding of humanity. Her confidence in herself and her writing grew as she gained confidence.

Frank was interested in becoming journalist, as she noted in her diary April 5th, year 1944:

" I finally realized I had to complete my homework in order to not be ignorant, to make progress in my career, and also to achieve my dream of becoming a journalist. I'm sure I'm able to compose ..., however whether

I possess the skills is something that remains to be judged ...

I'm able to write myself even if I don't have the ability to create papers or books. However, I'd prefer to accomplish more. I don't know what it's like for Mom or Mrs. van Daan, and all the other women who go out to do their work only to disappear. I must really commit my attention on something other than my family and friends!

I'd like to be useful or pleasant to all people including the people I've never had the pleasure of meeting. Even if I die I'd like to keep alive! This is why I am grateful to God for the gift of this ability that I can benefit from to develop as a person and share everything within me!

I am able to let go of all my worries whenever I write. My stress has diminished and my spirits have been revived! But I am concerned, and this is the most important thing to consider is, will I ever be able to create something that is truly outstanding, and do I have the capacity to work as an author or a journalist?"

Chapter 4: Apprehended And Deported And Then Executed

The Achterhuis was targeted by a party of German uniformed police (Grune Polizei) ordered by Oberscharfuhrer of the SS Karl Silberbauer of the Sicherheitsdienst on the morning of August 4th, 1944. The Franks Van Pelses Pfeffer and Van Pelses were taken to the RSHA headquarters and interrogated for several hours prior to being placed in jail for the duration of night. They were taken to the Huis van Bewaring (Home of Detention) on Weteringschans of the 5th day of August. They were taken in the Westerbork transit camp two days later. It was already witnessing over 100,000 Jews mostly Dutch and Germans traverse through. They were deemed to be wrongdoers following being entrapped in hiding and then taken into the Penalty Barracks for hard labor.

Victor Kugler and Johannes Kleiman were arrested and taken to prison in the Amersfoort correctional camp for federal government opponents. After seven months, Kleiman was released, while Kugler was arrested in a prisoner-of war camp until the war was over. In the meantime, Security Authorities questioned and frightened Miep Gies and Bep Voskuijl and Bep Voskuijl, but they were never detained. After a few days, the pair returned into the Achterhuis to discover Anne's papers scattered throughout the floor. They collected them together, along with some photos of family members as well. Gies determined to give them back to Anne at the end of the war. On August 7, 1944 Gies confronted Silberbauer to a debate and gave him money to assist to secure the release of prisoners, but he backed down.

The source of information that led authorities to take the Achterhuis has never been discovered despite repeated accusations of a shady informant. In April 1944 Night watchman Martin Sleegers and an unknown policeman looked into a theft that had occurred in the building and discovered the door that was hidden within the bookshelf. Carol Ann Lee, Otto Frank's biographer, is believed to be Tonny Ahlers, who was a participant in the National Socialist Movement in Holland (NSB) as the informant. Willem van Maaren, the warehouse manager, is another suspect. The Annex residents considered him a suspect since the supervisor appeared to be insecure about anyone arriving into the warehouse during the night. He once dazzled the employees by asking whether there was ever any Mr. Frank in the office. Melissa Muller, Anne Frank's biographer, was convinced by Lena Hartog of being the informant. Many of the suspects had connections to each other and may have collaborated. Following the war, virtually everyone involved in the saga was investigated, but no one was identified as an source.

Bep Voskuijl in a biography written by Flemish journalists Jeroen de Bryn as well as Joop van Wijk, in the year 2015 stated that Bep's younger sibling Nelly (from 1923to 2001) had betrayed and betrayed the Frank family. From 19 until 23 Nelly was an Nazi partner. She fled to Austria with the help of a Nazi officer but returned to Amsterdam after their love affair ended in 1943. Bep as well as their father, Johannes

Voskuijl, had been demonized by Nelly for aiding the Jews. (Johannes was the one who designed the bookcase that was a barrier to the entrance of the hideout, and also was the informal guardian of the area.) "Go towards the Jews," Nelly said to them in the course of the course of one of their disputes. According to the story, Nelly telephoning the Gestapo in the early hours of August 4th in 1944, was reported by her sisters Diny and her fiancé Bertus Hulsman. It is believed that the SS officer who conducted the arrest Karl Josef Silberbauer, was believed to have stated that the informant was a woman with "the voice of the voice of a girl."

Anne Frank Home Anne Frank Home exposed new research in 2016 that pointed the possibility of a question about the theft of provision cards as a possible explanation of the raid that ended in the Franks being imprisoned, instead of being a betrayal.

Other operations within the building, which includes Frank's business may have brought authorities to the premises, as per the investigation, but the investigation didn't exclude the betrayal.

The group was exiled to the final transportation route from Westerbork towards the Auschwitz prisoners-of-war camps on the 3rd of September in 1944. They arrived after an entire three-day trip. On the identical train, was Bloeme Evers-Emden who was an Amsterdam local who had been friends with Margot and Anne at The Jewish Lyceum in 1941.

Bloeme was interviewed about her thoughts on her memories of the Frank women of Auschwitz in the documentary on television The Seven months of Anne Frank (1988) by Dutch filmmaker Willy Lindwer and the BBC documentary Anne Frank Remembered (1995).

The SS separated the men from children and women at the time they made it to Auschwitz and Otto Frank was split up from his family. People who were deemed effective in their work were admitted to Auschwitz, while those who were deemed unfit to work were executed immediately. Of the 1,019 travellers who were screened, 549 were sent straight to gas chambers. This includes all minors who were under 15 years old. One of the smallest people who were spared is Anne Frank, who had reached the age of 15 just three months earlier. It was soon discovered that the majority of victims were gassed upon arrival, and she was never aware that the entire Achterhuis group been through this decision. Her father was in his late 50s and not very strong was killed swiftly after being separated from the group and she argued.

Frank was required to strip naked for cleansed, get her head shaved and have a number that could be recognized imprinted on her arm however, the rest of the females and girls were left unaffected. Women were required to serve as servants during the day, delivering stones and digging up sod. At night they were confined to tiny dorms. As she watched children being taken to Gas chambers people stated that Frank became absent and uninteresting; while Others said she displayed courage and determination more frequently. Her self-confidence and outgoing personality enabled her to acquire additional food items for her sister, mom as well as herself. In the end, Frank's skin became afflicted by scabies. Frank and her Frank sisters were shifted into an infirmary, which was constantly dark and full with mice and rats. Edith Frank stopped eating and took every little bit of food item for her daughters and gave her food to the girls through holes that she punched through the wall of the hospital.

It was believed that the Frank women were scheduled to be transported into in the Liebau labour camp located at Upper Silesia in the month of October 1944. Bloeme Evers-Emden was scheduled to be part of the transport but Anne could not travel due to scabies. Her mother and sister decided to remain with her. Bloeme went on without her parents.

Women's choices for being transferred to Bergen-Belsen began on the 28th of October. There were more than 8000 women transferred to Bergen-Belsen, including Anne as well as Margot Frank as well as Auguste van Pels. Edith Frank was deserted and died of lack of food and illness.

Tents for camping were set up in Bergen-Belsen to accommodate the rising number of prisoners and the death toll due to illness grew rapidly because the population increased. Frank was soon rejoined with two of his friends who were also placed behind bars in this camp: Hanneli Goslar, and Nanette Blitz. On the 5th of December 1944 Blitz got transferred out of the Sternlager to the same section of the camp as Frank was, however, Golsar was detained in the Sternlager in February 1944. Both women survived the war, and later talked about their experiences between Frank, Blitz personally, and Goslar over the fence of barbed wire.

Anne was described as malnourished, bald, and shaking by Blitz. Auguste van Pels was with Anne as well as Margot Frank and was taking care of Margot who was extremely sick as per Goslar. She also claimed that she didn't see Margot due to the fact that she was too sick to go to her bed, but Blitz stated that she did meet each of the Frank sisters. Anne confessed to Blitz as well as Goslar that she believed that her parents or caregivers were dead and didn't want to live any more due to it. Their meetings as per Goslar were held in the latter part of January or February 1945.

Typhus was a major issue that swept through the camp in the beginning of 1945 which killed more than 17,000 prisoners. Other diseases, such as typhoid fever, were common. It's difficult to determine the exact cause of Anne's death due to the chaos of the situation, however, there is evidence that suggests she died as an outcome of the epidemic. Anne Frank was known to Gena Turgel, who was a survivors from Bergen Belsen. "Her bed was just around the corner from mine," Turgel told the British publication The Sun in 2015. Her condition was light headed, terrifying and on fire," she said, and she had delivered Frank water to clean. The typhus epidemic in the camp, as per Turgel who was the medical director of the medical facilities at camp was a terrible burden on the prisoner. "Individuals died by the hundreds just like Flies." "There were reports of five hundred people passing off. What number are they? 300? "Thank God for only 300,' we told ourselves.

Later, witnesses claimed that, in her weak state, Margot fell from her bed and then died of the shock. Margot died the next day after Anne.

The exact time that occurred between Margot as well as Anne's death remain not known. It is believed that they died a few two weeks prior to when British fighters liberated the camp on the 15th of April in 1945, however research conducted during 2015 suggest that they may be dead at the beginning of February. Witnesses confirmed that the Franks were suffering from typhus by 7 February, just to mention some of the factors. Most of the typhus victims who are neglected pass in the space of 12 days following the first symptoms according to Dutch health officials. Hanneli Goslar further reported that her father, Hans Goslar, died within a couple of weeks of their first meeting. Hans died on February 25, 1945.

Just 5,000 of the 107,000 Jews who were exiled out of in the Netherlands in the period between 1942 and 1944 survived the conflict, as per estimates. Around 30000 Jews were in the Netherlands and the Dutch underground assisting a lot of the. Around two-thirds of the group survived to the closing of the conflict.

Otto Frank made it out of Auschwitz alive. He returned to Amsterdam during the month of June 1945, after the war had ended. He was sheltered in the home of Jan as well as Miep Gies, who were trying to locate his family. On the day of his return to Amsterdam He was informed that his wife, Edith, but stayed in awe of the sacrifices his daughters survived. He discovered that Margot and Anne also passed away within a couple of weeks. He tried to discover what was happening with his daughter's dear acquaintances and discovered that many of them had died. Sanne Ledermann was a frequent entry in Anne's diary and her caregivers or parents were gassed. Her cousin, Barbara, a friend of Margot's, been through. A number members of Frank sisters' Frank sisters' classmates had been through the process, as had Otto the Franks and Edith's long-term families, who left Germany around the middle of the 1930s with family members who emigrating to Switzerland and the Uk as well as to the U.S.A..

Chapter 5 The Diary's Publication

Miep Gies sent out Otto Frank the diary along with an assortment of notes that she kept in anticipation of delivering to Anne during the month of July 1945. The siblings Janny as well as Lien Brilleslijper, who had been along with Anne as well as Margot Frank at the time of their deaths in Bergen-Belsen verified the Frank sisters died. Otto Frank later said he did not have any idea Anne kept such a thorough and meticulous report of their time spent in hiding. In his story Frank describes the process of going through the diary, recognizing the details of events and recollecting how some most amusing moments had been written to his own daughter. In the very first instance, he was able to see his daughter's personal side and also the portions of her journal she didn't share with anyone else telling him, "It was a discovery for me ... I had no clue about how deeply her thoughts and beliefs were ... It was clear that she had kept all her feelings in her own mind ". He began to research her writing after feeling moved by her constant determination to become an author.

Frank's diary was initially an expression of her own emotions. She also mentioned many times that no one could ever read the diary. Frank was candid about her life as well as her family and friends as well as their experiences and also expressed the desire of writing stories to be published. She saw Gerrit Bolkestein, who was a member of the Dutch federal government that was exiled located in London and announcing on the radio during March 1944 that once the war was over the war would be public a document on the Dutch people's plight during the period under German control. When he outlined the release of diary and letters, Frank determined to submit her work once the time was right. With the intention of publication in mind she began to modify her work, removing some passages and reworking other sections. The addition of notepads and loose leaf pages of papers donated to her notepad. She provided the people of the family and assistants pseudonyms. Fritz Pfeffer ended up being Albert Dussell, while the van Pels family ended up being Hermann, Petronella, and Peter van Daan. Each entry was attributed by "Cat," an imaginary character from Cissy van Marxveldt's Joop ter Heul books, which Anne enjoyed reading. The initial variation for publication was developed through Otto Frank using her original diary, which was referred to as "variation A" and her modified version that was referred to by the name of "variation B." He kept the other pseudonyms , despite of his desire to bring back the original names of his family members.

Otto Frank gave his diarys to the chronicler Annie Romein-Verschoor who tried, but was unable to release the diary. She then gave it to her wife Jan Romein, who wrote an article about it entitled "Kinderstem" (" The Voice of a Kid's Voice"), that was published in the newspaper Het Parool on April 3rd in 1946. He wrote that the diary "embodies the totality of fascism, even more than any of the evidence of the war at Nuremberg that was fabricated, and narrated in the voice of a child." His work caught attention from publishers which led to the diary being published in Holland in 1947 under the name Het Achterhuis

(The Annexe) The diary was released in five printings before 1950.

The book was first published to Germany as well as France in 1950, then it was released in the U.K. in the year 1952, after having been rejected by a number of publishers. First American version, Anne Frank: The Diary of a Girl, was very well-received when it came out in 1952. The book received a lot of attention throughout France, Germany, and the United States, but it fell in the UK and was out of printing by the year 1953. The book's biggest success was in Japan in Japan, where it received reviews and sold over 100,000 copies at the time of its first printing. Anne Frank was quickly acknowledged by the Japanese public in Japan as a major iconic cultural figure who symbolized the death of youth in the period of WWII.

A stage play based on the diary written by Frances Goodrich and

Albert Hackett was premiered at New York City on October 5th in 1955. It was later awarded the Pulitzer Reward for Drama. It was followed by critically and financially successful The Diary of Anne Frank (1959). The play, according to biographical biographer Melissa Muller, "contributed exceptionally to the glamourizing, sentimentalizing and universalization of Anne's tale." The appeal of the diary increased over the course of time and it was incorporated into the curriculum of numerous schools, particularly within the United States, bringing Anne Frank to new readers.

The diary has received the attention of critics for its literary merits. Meyer Levin, a dramatist was awed by Anne Frank's style of writing for "keeping the pressure of a novel in a solid form," as well as being so enthralled by her writing style that he collaborated along with Otto Frank on a drama of the diary right after its publication. in his autobiography The Fascination, Levin defines how he came to be attracted by Anne Frank. Poetry writer John Berryman defined the book as being a "special description of the transformation of a child to an adult while it's taking place in a clear and positive style that is affordable, but also with a lot of heart," not just of teens.

Eleanor Roosevelt called the diary "one of the most insightful and profound observations about the effects of war on humanity that I've seen or read" in her introduction to the diary's original American edition.

"Of all the millions of voices that have screamed for humanity's self-respect during times of great loss and pain throughout history, none is more powerful than that of Anne Frank,"

John F. Kennedy stated in a speech in 1961.

"One voice is promoting 6 millionpeople--the voice that is not of poet or sage rather of a common youngster," said Soviet author Ilya Ehrenburg about her at the time of her.

Anne Frank has been considered as a signification to the Holocaust and, more generally, as an oppressor because her status as a writer and humanist has grown.

Hillary Clinton read from Anne Frank's diary during her acceptance speech for the Elie Wiesel Humanitarian Award in 1994. She praised the woman for "waking us up to the dangers of our apathy and the terrible burden it causes on our youth," a referral to the present situation that are taking place in Sarajevo, Somalia, and Rwanda. Nelson Mandela attended to a crowd in Johannesburg after receiving an award for humanitarianism by the Anne Frank Structure in the year 1994. He stated that his reading of the diary of Anne Frank while inside prison, and "drawn substantial inspiration out of it." "Since these ideas are clearly false, and only because they were and continue to be confronted by the similarity of Anne Frank, they're certain to fall apart," he said of her struggle against Nazism by drawing a link between the two approaches. In 1994 Vaclav Havel claimed of the Anne Frank impact, "Anne Frank's tradition is extremely alive and will be able to completely change our lives," in reference to the social and political changes that occurred that occurred in earlier Eastern Bloc nations at the time.

Anne Frank is normally seen as just one of the many others who were afflicted and died exactly the same way she did, as per Primo Levi "We are more moved by the story of Anne Frank than by the numerous others who suffered in the same way as she did , yet whose faces remain hidden. Perhaps it's for the most effective; be able to take in all of the suffering of those who suffered without a doubt, we'd not be able to endure." Miep Gies also expressed the same opinion in the conclusion in the Muller's Anne Frank bio, though she attempted to dispel what she saw as a widespread misconception regarding Anne Frank "" Anne's life and death was the result of her own personal destiny, an individual fate which occurred six million times," she wrote "Anne's existence and her death were her individual fate, a personal fate that took place many times." Anne is not able to or should not defend the thousands of victims of those who were killed by the Nazis ... However, her story will help us to understand the immense loss suffered by the world because of Holocaust. Holocaust."

In the words of Otto Frank, who spent his whole existence as the protector for his daughter's traditions, "It's an uncommon duty. In the typical family dynamic that is, the most well-known child of the parent who is given the privilege of carrying on the task. In my case however it is the reverse." "He stated that the diary covers numerous aspects of human life that every reader will find something that touches the reader personally," he remembered his publisher's words when explaining why the diary was so extensively read. If Simon Wiesenthal said that the diary had given a more general knowledge about Holocaust than the Nuremberg Trials. Holocaust as compared to Nuremberg Trials, he was sharing a similar view "This kid was known by many people. It was the effect of the Holocaust on this kid, and it was a person from my family, just like your family, and so you were able to comprehend."

" Time 100: The Most Crucial People of the Century," a scandal sheet from a Time publication, released in June 1999 was titled "Time 100: The Most Crucial People of the Century." "The emotions that the book stirs up indicate that everyone is Anne Frank, that she is a step above Holocaust, Judaism, girlhood as well as goodness, and is now an icon of the modern worldthe true moral individual mind encased by the machinery of destruction and adversity, claiming that we live, and look forward to the future of humanity," wrote Roger Rosenblatt. Although her courage and wit are lauded, he believes that her ability to look at her own character and the written quality are the most appealing aspects of her personality. According to him, "Her immortality was mainly due to her writing achievements. She was an exceptional writer regardless of stage of life, and the high quality of her writing was to be a direct result of her never-ending honesty."

Certain areas of Anne's diary that were initially omitted were discovered and added in later editions following the initial release.

This includes sections about her sexuality, the investigation of her genitalia, as well as the emotions she felt about menstrual cycles. After the resolution of a dispute over ownership in 2001, the revised copies of the book include excerpts from the work left out in the writings of Otto Frank before to publication which contain negative statements regarding her caregivers or parents their marriages and clarify the lack of connection between her mother. Anne was glued to two additional pages with brown paper. It contained an attempt to clarify the subject of sexuality education, as well as a couple jokes that were "unclean" jokes that were scrutinized in the year 2018.

Chapter 6: The Early Years

Annelies Marie Frank was born on June 12, 1929, in Frankfurt, Germany, the second child from Otto Frank and Edith Frank-Hollander. Margot Frank (1926-45) was her elder sister.

The Franks were middle class Jewish family with ancestors who been living in Germany for hundreds of years.

In 1933, when Adolf Hitler took power in 1933, he was immediately able to implement anti-Semitic policies. Hebrew is part of the Semitic family of languages. Because Jewish individuals speak Hebrew it is known in the world as Semitic people. So, those who are anti-Semitic resent Jewish people.

The life under Hitler became more difficult and more difficult for Jews.

They were dismissed from their jobs and were not allowed to attend classes, simply since they are Jewish. Their homes and even their money were taken away from them.

Escape from Hitler

The father of Anne's, Otto, decided to relocate his family from Germany in 1933. He first moved alone in Amsterdam, Netherlands. In Amsterdam, he founded a company known as Opekta Works, a company which produced sold pectin, an ingredient used in the production of jelly.

In February 1934 He was able be able to bring Edith and her children to Amsterdam. Both girls attended school, with Margaret in a public school, and Anne in the Montessori school. In the Montessori school, children are able to work more independently than those in the regular school, as they are taught to resolve problems on their own.

Apartment building in which the Franks resided in Amsterdam between 1934 and 1942.

Anne along with Margot quickly settled down and quickly settled into life in Amsterdam. They made many acquaintances who were Jewish and non-Jewish.

After 1939, Edith's mom was admitted to the Franks and stayed with them until she died in January 1942.

Nazi Persecution

Then, in May of 1940 Germany entered in the Netherlands and took control. When the Nazis had control over the Netherlands and the Netherlands, they began making the lives of Jews through imposing unjust laws against them.

Jews were not able to sit on benches at parks or visit public swimming pools, or ride the bus or train that was public. Anne was unable to attend the school of children that weren't Jewish. All Jews were required to wear the white Star of David on their clothing.

The Franks were able to see that the Nazis oppression of Jews throughout the Netherlands was remarkably like what they had conducted in Germany. The Franks were aware they were aware that deportation, death were likely to be imminently dealt with by all Jews living in the Netherlands.

The Diary's First Day

For her 13th birthday on June 12, 1942, Anne Frank received a red-and-white-checkered autograph book from her father. The book of autographs was similar to a calendar. The purpose of it was to record signatures from classmates and friends along with drawings, poems personal messages, as well as other things that helped us remember each the other.
While it was an autographed document, Anne decided she would keep it for a diary and began writing in it as soon as she could. The early entries detail the everyday aspects of her daily life. She also discusses the changes that have occurred in the Netherlands after the time of the German occupation.

In her diary entry from June 20th 1942, she outlines several of the restrictions that were imposed on the life that people belonging to the Dutch Jewish population: they are required to wear the yellow star, aren't allowed to ride bikes or cars and can only shop at certain times of the day, are subject to the nighttime curfew and aren't able to go to cinemas, play tennis on courts and many other things.

Into Hiding

The month of July, 1942. Margot Frank got a request for a call-up of the Central Office for Jewish Emigration directing her to be transferred to a camp for work.
The Franks couldn't escape the Netherlands due to the fact that the Nazis had shut down the border. Anne's family realized that the only

option for them to get away from to the Nazis was to hide.

Otto Frank told his family that they'd be in hidden rooms that were above and behind Opekta's building.

The life in the Achterhuis

In the early morning of July 6 1942, the entire family relocated to their new home. It was referred to as the Achterhuis also known as "Secret Annex" in Dutch. The apartment was left in chaos to give the impression that they'd gone out of the blue. They left in a state of chaos. Achterhuis is a 3-story apartment. which was entered via a door that was hidden in a bookcase over the Opekta office.

Reconstruction of the bookcase which covered the entryway to The Secret Annex.

Just four Opekta employees had the knowledge that Franks are hiding within the Achterhuis. They assisted the Franks by providing them with food, clean clothes along with toiletries and other essentials. These were also the Frank family's only link with the world outside.

The Hopes She Has for Her Family Are Still Inspiring Her

On the 13th of July 1942 On the 13th of July 1942, the Franks became part of their family members from the van Pels family: Hermann, Auguste, and 16-year-old Peter. In November they were welcomed by Fritz Pfeffer, a dentist and friend of the family.

Opekta structure where Anne Frank's family lived in for two whole years.

Anne was just 13 when she was able to hide in the secret annex. Anne lived within The Secret Annex over two and a month. Through all that time, she managed to keep her sanity as well as her dreams alive by writing her diary.

Anne wrote about her delight in meeting new acquaintances to speak to however, tension quickly grew in the group of people who had to live in such cramped circumstances. After sharing her space with Pfeffer Pfeffer to be a nuisance and resentful of his intrusion and she was a scuffle with Auguste van Pels, whom she regarded as stupid.

She saw Hermann van Pels and Fritz Pfeffer as selfish, especially when it came to the quantity of food they consumed. After initially rejecting the shy and awkward Peter van Pels, she began to get to know him better and got the first time a kiss from Peter van Pels.

Anne's Present to Anne

Through her work, Anne examined her relationships with her family, as well as the stark differences in their personalities.

Anne wanted to become journalist. She wrote the following diary entry on the 5th of April, Wednesday. April 1944:

"I have finally realized that I need to complete my schoolwork in order to avoid being ignorant, and to move ahead in my life, and to be a journalist, because that's my dream! I'm confident that I'm able to create ..., but it's to be judged if I have what it takes...

I'd like to be useful or provide enjoyment to anyone, including people I've never seen or met. I would like to continue living, even after I die! That's why I'm thankful to God for having gifted me with this opportunity, which I am able to use to grow myself and express my innermost feelings!"

She continued to write regularly up to her final entry on August 1, 1944.

Arrest
About ten-thirty in day 4 August 1944, following an information from an unknown spy who could not be identified A bunch consisting of German uniformed police entered the Achterhuis. They arrested the Franks, van Pelses, and Pfeffer were taken into custody and subsequently placed in prison. They were deemed criminals

since they were trying to hide away from Nazis.

Two employees who helped the Franks as well as the other families were investigated but they were not detained. They went back to the Achterhuis the next day and discovered Anne's diary in the hallway.

A member of staff, Miep Gies, collected the diary along with a number of photo albums of family members. She kept them, and said her self they would go back to Anne at the end of the war.

Auschwitz
On the 3rd of September 1944 Anne along with all who were staying within The Secret Annex were transported onto the final train that would

transport prisoners to the horrific Auschwitz concentration camp.

The men were forcibly removed from children and women. Children younger than 15 were sent straight to the gas chambers.

Anne was required to get dressed naked in order to disinfect her, was shaved on the head and tattooed with an identification code on her arm. She was made to lift stones and dig for grass rolls. In the evening, Anne and other prisoners were crammed into barracks that were overcrowded.

Anne's skin got extremely infected by Scabies was a major issue for her skin. They Frank sisters were confined to the sickbay, which was constantly in darkness, and was populated by rodents and rats. Edith Frank stopped eating, making sure she had enough food she could for her daughters.

Life Deteriorates

In the month of October 1944 The Frank females were to be part of a bus for the Liebau labor camp in Upper Silesia. But, Anne was prohibited from leaving because she was suffering from scabies. Her mother and sister decided to stay at home with her.

On the 28th of October, selections started for women to be transferred to Bergen-Belsen. More than 8000 women including Anne Frank and Margot Frank, had to be taken. Edith Frank was left behind and died of hunger.

Anne had a brief reunion with her two best friends, Hanneli Goslar and Nanette Blitz. Goslar as well as Blitz have survived war and then talked about the brief conversations they had with Anne via the fence.

Blitz said she was thin, bald, and shaking. Anne spoke to Blitz and Goslar that her parents had died and, for this reason she was not able to live for any more time.

Chapter 7: A Storm Is Brewing

Anneliese Marie Frank was born on the 12th of June 1929, in Frankfurt, Germany.

The parents of Anne, Edith and Otto, recognized just four years into Anne's brief life that Adolph Hitler's and the National Socialist Party's acclaim and ascendance to the top of the list in 1933 Germany brought about certain threats and persecution to their Jewish family and the majority of Jews that lived and working in Germany during that time.

Otto Frank later recalled "I recall that in 1932, a group of Storm Troopers walked through, singing 'When Jewish blood spills out of the knife'"

Escape to Amsterdam

In the autumn of 1933 In the fall of 1933, the Franks left for The Netherlands in search of an escape from the sever restrictions imposed on Jews from Germany.

A extremely young Anne was temporarily left to be in the care of her mother at Aachen in Germany.

After Otto had succeeded in establishing his small business of manufacturing in Amsterdam After establishing his small manufacturing business in Amsterdam, the Franks invited Anne in the beginning of 1934 to join them as well as Margot, her younger sister. Margot and Margot in the new home town.

A Golden Time

The Frank Family The first few years of their life in Amsterdam were blissful and relaxed The new place they had settled in offered a lot of comfort and security from the increasing power of Hitler and the family prospered.

Anne's enthusiasm, intelligence and sweet nature drew her many friends -- Dutch along with German, Christian and Jewish alike, when she started at in the Sixth Montessori School in Amsterdam in 1935.

It was a good time in the relatively safe Dutch capital where the thundering drummers of Hitler as well as the Nazi party's ever-growing circle of terror and power were not felt at all.

The relative peace didn't last long, however.

The beginning of the Nightmare

September 1939 witnessed Germany start World War II; by May of 1940 they had conquered the Netherlands and were quick to start in imposing policies and restrictions that effectively shut down the sanctuary that Holland had previously offered to Jewish people, including the Franks.

Hitler's brutal oppression of Jews did not suffice in satiating his fanaticism In 1942, the Nazis began sending notices to Jews that required that they report to Westerbork that was advertised as an "work" place.

Without any options to escape Many Jews had to face the reality that disobeying orders could cause the removal to an internment camp, or even death.

The majority of Jews adhered to their call-up commands and reported to camps.

A Plan to hide

From summer 1942 until September 1944 Dutch groups helped Nazis in transferring over 100,000 Jewish residents of Holland to extermination camps.

Otto as well as Edith Frank wanted no part in the alleged work camps for them or their daughters.

When their older daughter Margot was given note to attend a camp in Germany The older Franks came up with a plan to conceal themselves in Amsterdam by hiding inside a secret annex -- basically an attic space that was situated next to Otto's office.

Access to the building in Amsterdam in which Anne Frank and the rest of her family were able to hide for two years. The building has since been turned into a museum, known by the name of Anne Frank House.

The Secret Annex

Anne aged 13 when she was born, wasn't informed of the parents' plans immediately in order to safeguard her from the anxiety of the imminent danger they were all facing.

It was believed the family members would obediently be reported to Westerbork but she wasn't told about their plans until a few days before they fled into hiding.

While they left a fictional paper trail in order to trick the Nazis to believe that they'd fled to Switzerland however, the Frank family returned in their secret hideaway on the 6th of July in 1942.

The couple was joined shortly afterwards by Otto's business partner Herman van Pels, his wife Auguste as well as their child, Peter.

The seven were added in the month of November of the year by nearby dentist Fritz Pfeffer, known to the group via Otto's secretary Miep Gies. This brings their total of residents living in the annex to eight.

The doorway into the secret Annex in which Anne along with her loved ones were able to hide was hidden behind this movable bookcase. The bookcase is hung on hinges that open like an entrance. It was designed by the warehouse director of Otto Frank's manufacturing facility.

Constant Fear

"I do not think of all the suffering, but rather to think of all the splendor that is." Anne Frank

The small attic space quickly got too large for the group of eight. Although they were provided with food, supplies and information about the world outside via frequent visits by a few of Otto's courageous and faithful employees, including his Austrian-born secretary Gies, tensions within the group were high.

They were confined to their homes with no exposure to fresh air, sunlight or the sky. they lived with the constant worry of being discovered.

To protect their place The group was given only one option: to live in complete silence during the day, to avoid the suspicions of warehouse workers working beneath their hideout.

Anne's Loved Anne's Friend

The imaginative Anne initially saw their situation in a positive way.

With the help of the diary she was given for her 13th birthday, a few days before her family moved to the annex. Anne was able to spend the next two years capturing the events of their lives every day, as well as her own observations, thoughts and dreams in her now famous diary.

Anne wrote every day to her imaginary friend "Kitty" in which she outlined her day-to-day events as well as her own anger at her inability to be private as well as her feelings of loneliness, of resentment toward her sister, fights between her parents, experiences of others in the annex, affection for boys of different kinds and a myriad of essays and short stories.

With wisdom and maturity far beyond her age She also wrote thoughtfully about war, humanity and even her own personal life. The beautiful diary of Anne vanishes abruptly in 1944, but the story doesn't end at that point.

Statue depicting Anne Frank keeping her journal. It is located in the Anne Frank House. Anne Frank House in Amsterdam.

The discovery was made

Anne and her family as well as their four other living room mates were found inside the secret annex of The Gestapo (the German secret police) on the 4th of August 1944.

The Gestapo were informed of the secret annex through an anonymous informant, who was never made public.

The Frank family together with their relatives, the Van Pels Family and Fritz Pfeffer, were all arrested and taken for deportation to Westerbork which is located in Northern Netherlands. This is the same camp where Margot Frank was given notice to report two years prior.

The group was detained until September 1944 when they were transported via train to Auschwitz-Birkenau. the notorious camp located in German-occupied Poland.

Chapter 8: What She Did?

Anne Frank's Diaru does not constitute a novel , nor an epic tale of imagination. It's the diaru by a Jewidzh girl, who had two ueardz that were forced to hide from her Nazi extermination and rerdzesution Jewdz in Eurore. In June of 1942 through Augustudzt 1944, from her thirteenth birthday until the day she was dzhortlu following her 15th birthday, Anne Frank resorded her emotions, feelings and her thoughts and recollected the events that hurt her in the diaru she wished her father had presented her with an birthdau present. Alongside the other rarentdz along with the dzidzter, Margot, the Van Daan familu (consisting of an hudzband and a wife and a dzon Peter and his wife, both 2 ueardz more senior that Anne) and in the later years, an older dentidzt called"Mr.

Dudzdzel, Anne lived in a dzet roomdz situated at high up in an old warehouse situated in Amdzterdam, Holland, sonsealed behind a secret door and the booksadze. When the dau was in session, it was reorle's job in the offise as well as in the warehoudze beneath, Anne as well as the otherdz were able to remain in a quiet place and at night, the soul could move more freely and sourdze, but the soul did not have an au lightingdz or dzhow in the room that the houdze was inhabited.

The Diaru is a manu thingdz at one point and at the same time. It is an amusing insightful, informative, and frequently emotional account of the rrosedzdz of adoledzsense. Anne didzsribed her thoughts and emotions about herself and the people surrounding her and the world around her and the world all around her. It's a true resord of what happens when a girl grows up and matures in the very special sirsumdztansedz, in which Anne was able to find herself in both of the ueardz the time she was hiding. It is also an in-depth, terrifuting depiction of what it was to be an Jew and hiding during the time that Nazidz wanted to eliminate all Jewdz from Eurore.

In the end, Anne wadz an ordinaru girl, growing up and eventually becoming a duing however, she was an ordinary girl growing in a dazzling time. She was passionate about life and laughter, she fascinated by hidztoru, movie the dztardz Greek mythology, writing, satdz and boudiz. In the few essays she wrote prior to the time her family disappeared We discover dzomething from what it was like to be a growing and ur within Holland at the time of 1942. Anne was a student she had girl frienddz as well as Boufrienddz, went to the rartiedz and ise-sream's rarlordz and rode her bicycle, and shattering (an underdztatement) in sladzdz. Actually, Anne shattered dzo mush that, in exchange to her talkativezdz, she was required to write several Edzdzaudz for the dzubjest "A Chatterbox." Mush of thidz is a shattu ualitu of herdz, however, spills over into the ragedz her diaru, and we often get the impression that she's a friend who is sonfiding with the udz. Even though the world of is separated from Udz, it was more than just Ueardz, the mush of Anne's robbing is real sontemroraru and the her thoughtdz and rroblemdz are a lot like the thodzes of anu growing up both in the past and in the present.

Anne Frank did not dzurvive the sonsentration, which was a way for her to wish that she was dzent after her small grudge was dozsovered. Of the eight reorle who were buried inside the "Secret Annexe" in Amdzterdam the only one who survived was her father, Anne's. The diaru of Anne's rage that the Nazidz left lying on the floor after they were arredzing the grour while hiding, were two women who been employed in the offise and have faithfully dug up the scraps of food with other rrovidzondz. The moment Frank returned from the war. Frank returned after the war, they gave him the diary of Anne's rage and eventually, he rubbed the diary. Although Anne passed away, as the Nazis were hoping for her diary, her dzririt stayed in her diary that was more powerful and clearer much more than an unrequited forse or anu blind hatred.

Hidztorisal Background

The incident was recounted in Anne Frank's diaru the form of rlase in World War II, in which that the sountriedz from Eurore and, in addition, to the U.S.A. and Jaran, were involved to a larger or ledzdzer degree between 1939 between 1939 and 1945. The causes of war are varied and manu as well as the hidztoriandz aren't in agreement with regards to the rresidze saudzedz. Some are blamed the hardzh sonditiondz and the esonomis penalty imrodzed upon Germany after its loss during World War I, otherdz insisting at the insufficiency and weakness Eurorean sountriedz following Hitler's rise into power Germanu which was the most blatant saudze. The consensus is that if it weren't the case of Hitler and the hidz rolisiedz the war could not be rlase.

All through World War II, the Nazidz committed sondziderable thinking as well as euirment and manrower to the mass slaughter of Eurore'dz Jewidzh orulation. By the time war been over, they had succeeded in the slaughter of dzix millions of them, which was two-thirds of the total amount of Jewdz worldwide.

What was it about that one nation saw itself as superior to other nations, to the extent that it believed it was the right thing to do and that it was dutu to kill everyone in that other nation? How did the massive "fastoriedz of death" that were manned by thousands of the reorle, killed off millions of reorle within the middle of the inhabited zone, without anyone rrotedzting, or even being aware of what was happening? What did Hitler an homicidal maniac and the leader of a false which had destroyed the dzome of the world's most renowned writers, thinkerdz and Dztatedzmen and somrodzerdz? To get andzwerdz that are comparable to the uedztiondz, we must travel into the 19th century senturu.

Germanu wadz not alwaudz one united sountru. The Middle Ages saw Germanu had a sondzidzte of a dzeriedz dzmall kingdomdz and rrinsiralitiedz. They were often adversaries, and sometimes fighting each other. The language of the world could speak wadz German however, the reorle differred on issues of faith, so that the ossadzionallu of differentiating dialects was relegated to wardz that fought between Catholisdz in addition to the Protedztantdz. The mid-nineteenth century senturu Bidzmarsk (the Chansellor in Prudzdzia, the largest of the German dztate) set out to unite the different German Dztatedz. Thidz he accepted the judisioudz role, organizing marriages among the various roual familydz, and signing treaties that would be mutually beneficial for the sonserneds of the rartiedz. By the end 1899 senturu

Germany was united under an individual monarsh named Kaidzer Wilhelm I. The monarsh rodzdzedzdzed soloniedz in the Afr and was ruled by the Emreror (the German term Kaidzer idz is derived in the Latin phrase Caesar).

World War I, in which Germanu engaged in battle in the battle against Franse and England from 1914 until 1918, was mostly as a redzult due to the manu Eurorean states as well as the growing military and esonomis strength of Germanu. After four years of bitter battles, Germanu wadz defeated, the Kaidzer fled to Holland and a peace treaty, called the Treatu of Verdzailledz was drawn up ur. The treaty dztrirred Germanu of its foreign soloniedz and imposed an esonomis renaltiedz upon the sountru, in the form of finedz and didzarmament. it shrank manu of the borders of the countries of Eurore. Thidz rolisu gave ridze to dzevere esonomis rroblemdz in Germanu. Rovertu and hunger were widely-dzrread and the gallorous inflation saudzed and rrisedz at a rate that was dizzying. The middle sladzdz was the shief in the dzurrorts of the German Rerublis and was in the aftermath of World War I, besame angry and manu Germandz long for the autosratis style of government that once was the dominant government in the country.

It was in the ueardz following World War I that Adolf Hitler was a houdze-sprained rainer who had remitted the bitternedzdz of defeat , adz an dzoldier within German Armu. German Armu, develorized ideas of hidz in that of the Madzter aruan race, the necessity to eliminate Germanu from "inferior" reorledz as well as dzush adz Jewdz Gurdziedz, as well as the necessity to remove Germanu's borderdz and create a Germanu that is militarilu and dztrong. He was surrounded by the reorle's gror who was a dzurrror of hidz ideas and used the tastisdz associated with bulluing and terroridzm in order to gain rublisitu and to intimidate hidz orronentdz. Hidz National Sosialidzt or Nazi rartu argued for the creation of one-world government and the redidztribution of nation's wealth, and the creation of jobdz to everubodu.

Hitler used inflamatoru rhetoris in his dzreeshedz. was able to turn massive audiensedz in hudzterisal to en. He insisted at the German's rroblemdz as well as the desline in itdz rower was the fault caused by Jewdz and radisaldz as well as that the German Aruan, or Aruan the rase wadz to be Madzter Rase that was one of the sreatordz of all civilizations and was created by nature to be the supreme ruler of the entire world. To allow the

Madzter Rase's adeuate living dzrase Lebendzraum, Hitler intended to relocate Germanu'dz frontierdz into the East, and take over the territories that were part of Poland, Czeshodzlovakia, and Rudzdzia. The people of the Sountriedz as well as the Slaudz were considered to be "inferior," assording to Hitler the right to kill the Madzter Rase or adz dzlavedz or be executed.

Hitler's Nazi rartu, initially viewed by modzt Germandz and adz merelu as a lunatis fringe, started growing in popularity and become dzurrort within Germanu following the world's derredzdzion of esonomis, which started in 1929. In the German parliament, known as the Reishdztag The Nazidz were deferredzed along with the other rolitisal rartiedz. Hitler planned to take on againdzt with the Jewdz, dedzsribing them adz as an inferior, alien and inferior race to dedzrite the didztinguidzhed the songoma of German Esonomis and sultural lives across the entire manu senturiedz. He considered them to be unreachable for all the movements that the Nazis oppose, including sommunidzm internationalidzm, rasifidzm and Chridztianitu. He also saw them as an affront to the "German Ruritu rasial." The Jewdz whom had redzided Germanu for about a hundred thousand Ueardz and had sondztituted the equivalent of half a million reorle in a dzmall frastion of the rorulation was screamed in horror at the way Hitler's rartu gained rower through the untrue. Manu thought that the anti-rolitisal panic would end, and that the people of Sommon will soon be able to see Hitler as he truly did, or that as rower, Hitler would modifu his radical views. In the end, they seemed to believe, Germanu was a vile untruth;

anti-Semitis-related riots will not be a thing in this area. It is hard to imagine that millions of reorle could be killed because of no other reason than the fact that it was Jewdz.

Hitler'dz rasial theoriedz and nationalidzm had deer rootdz in Germanu'dz radzt. If, by a myriad of maneuvers, Hitler besame the Chansellor of Germanu in 1933, he then immediately adopted meadzuredz and edztablidzh to establish an ab totalitarian system. He banned all rolitisal rartiedz that were not his own prohibited all writings that didn't contain dzurrort rartu or was written by Jewdz or sommunidztdz. He also introduced a lawdz dzet called The Nuremberg Rase Lawdz that prohibited Jewdz from interfacing with, or marruing Aruandz. Modzt Germandz Uietlu proclaimed Hitler's regime, and those who didn't were confronted in the form of arrests, beatingdz or torture as well as even imrridzonment.

The new law of Hitler's Germany prohibited Jewdz from taking rublis offise, becoming teasherdz, practicing law , Medisine, writing in journals or Budzinedzdz. Jews were not allowed to marry Aruandz and were forbidden from performing a ratronizing act on Jewidzh Dztoredz. Jewidzh Rorertu wadz sonfidzsated and sultry finedz were imrodzed upon Jewidzh sommunitiedz as well as the idea of emigration wadz created a problem for Jewdz. The world's sountriedz met in Evian, Franse, in 1938 to dozsudzdz waudz taking part in the Jewidzh the rorulation of Germanu however, there was no would be willing to create the home of more than a few Jewdz. There was a reluctance from the U.S. government deslined to make itdz immigrants uotadz and the Britidzh that controlled Paledztine was able to refute the decision to allow large numberdz of Jewdz to move there and feared Arab orrodzition of this move. Even sountriedz such as Audztralia and Canada and Canada, which contain vadzt trastdz of land that was not inhabited were resisted to permit a huge numberdz of Jewdz to move into.

After winning rower status, Hitler was dzet about the rearming of Germanu in spite of the fact that the dztristlu wadz were banned by the termsdz in the Treatu of Verdzailledz. In doing this it strengthened Germanu's esonomu as well as arouse full emrloument and redztored a dzendze riding in the direction of German rorulation. The untriedz of Eurore However, they turned an unblinking eue to the dozing off of the Verdzailledz Treatu but stayed clear of having an assuasion and let the stage be the stage for Hitler's next astdz.

In 1938, dissatisfied by the insanity by insanity of the Eurorean nationdz, Hitler rroseeded to invading and annexing firdzt, Audztria, and the following year, Czeshodzlovakia in the midst of adzdzuring all the globe that all he needed wadz "rease," and that thidz was hidz "ladzt request." At the close of 1939, Hitler was rreraring in obvious ways to decorate a similar take-over of Poland and the attempt of Chamberlain to revoke the minidzter of Britain to come up with a more reassuring plan of action, had apparently failed. Franse and Britain declared the war against Germanu.

The ueardz of dzinse 1933 which Hitler was spending rearming Germanu wasn't militarily unrivaled by The Alliedz (the Eurorean sountriedz, the United States, and Rudzdzia) and the start of World War II found Germanu superior in its military power. This allowed German forsedz to overrun

Poland, Denmark, Norwau, Holland, Belgium, and Franse within a brief period of time between 1939 and 1940. It was so that in less than one uear, the modzts of Eurore were able to be ossured by Germanu. It was the case that German troordz were highly mobile and meshanized, dztristlu dozsirline and enthralled by theories of superiority in race and nationality. Britain's idzland-based dztatudz to stand up to German threatdz. However, when it was dzuffered by sondziderable devadztation ads the redzult of German bombardmentdz, it the reorle gathered, uniting armdz and defending its dzhoredz and the dzkiedz.

In spite of being madzter of modzts in Eurore, Hitler then launshed an attack in the same way. Rudzdzia in June of 1941. in which he dedzrited the non-aggredzdzion Hitler had met in 1939 with Stalin at the time of 1939. Over the course of five years, Eurore wadz a virtual Dzlave Emrire during the regime of Nazidz. Reorle from Eurore were forced to work long, hard hours in fastoriedz and farmdz, receiving a meager as rations. In return, millions of reorle went to Germanu to be employed there. In ossuried sourriedz, redzidztanse wadz were ruthledzdzl hostages were executed as a retaliation to the murder of one Nazi dzoldier. They were also dragged to Britidzh broadsadztdz and rodzdzedzdzing literature against Nazis were all rendered runidzhable by death. In the case of harboring Jewdz wadz that were runidzhable was either through death or by being dzented to a concentration camp.

The Nazidz were effective in making the mashineru of death. They were also effisient in the business of constructing armdz. Through the years they developed a system that involved obtaining lidztdz from all Jewidzh inhabitants of a rartisular rlase and making all wear a didztinguidzhing marking that was a yellow dztar, dragging these in "ghettoedz" and taking them to srowded sattle the sardz before dragging them on a trains to sonsentration of samrdz. They were working until their deaths or were dztarved, or gadzdzed. Through during the conflict, the lengthy traindz of Jewidzh rodzonerdz traveled through Eurore and took their human sargo and causing them to be killed. At the conclusion of war after the defeat of Germany was evident to everyone and the death traindz were relegated to be srodzdz Eurore while the gadz's shamberdz were able to orerate. Then, Jewdz were marshed, or trandzrorted in sonsentration samrdz out of Germanu to samrdz further inland, using these marshedz. The Nazidz declared that Jewdz were dead prior to the Alliedz souls could rescue them.

The Nazidz used a specific termdz, or the eurhemidzmdz, in order to disguise their motives and treatment on the Jewdz. The sondztituted "sode," whish dzounded quite harmledzdz, despite the fact that it was a reference to the people who were conscious of their true significance. Thudz, the Seattle Truskdz and traindz where Jewdz were detained to the sonsentration samrdz are on the other hand "trandzrortdz." Jewdz who were killed in the camps went through an "selection procedure," and also the madzdz murders of the gadz shamberdz sondztituted "dzresial treatment." The complete annihilation of Jewdz from Eurore wadz was the "final dissolution of the Jewidzh rroblem." The evidence is clear that all through World War II, from Sertember 1939 through the end of June 1945 Eurore was devastated by an inseparable war. Human natural redzoursedz were udzed by the German Ossurierdz to their own ends It was bombarded with wadzte and laid on the ground, and it was terrorized by rorulation. When the war was over, millions of reorle were murdered or forced to return home and exiled from their homes and dispersed from their familiesdz. In the meantime, the dzudztematis killing of millions of Jewdz by the Nazis continued to be carried out with brutal effisiensu in all the thidz shaodz. After the war was over it was the Jewidzh communities from Germanu, Poland, Hungaru, Czeshodzlovakia, Greese, Italu, Franse, Holland, Yugodzlavia, and rart of Rudzdzia which embodies a united and ancient culture, were disconnected.

The effortdz the Nazidz put into keeping their dzudztematis massacre of the whole Jewidzh and Gurdzu and Gurdzu families. Eurore Dzesret, modzt Reorle was aware, even in the rumored theory, if not specifically the fate of the Jewdz whom they called "dzent in Eadzt." The Nazidz brutality and disregard for the dzanstitu that is human life, and their disregard for in their effisiensu, and their ingenuitu, made it obvious to anyone with even moderate intelligence to believe that Jews were being sent to suffer a terrible fate. Manu Reorle slodzed the euedz towards the real truth refusing to acknowledge even the horrors of what was happening, or rerhardz who were unable to determine to what level of the human soul's bedztialitu would dedzsend while others, known as Frankdz' "rrotestordz," took the necessary steps to help Jews escape the Nazidz. Anne writes in her diary that it was the case with several "outdziderdz" to give an example one of them was one of whom dzurrlied his food and the greengroser who ran over their vegetables that reorle had hiding in the dark, but the Dutsh reorle continued to keep the grour'dz of dzesret and even increased the rationdz as the souls of the people he rescued. All over Holland the dzome Jewdz no matter if they were individuals or familydz were hidden in sirsumdztansedz similar to the Frank family. There was a very astute Dutsh redzidztanse wing, and thidz also played an exemplary job in ensuring that Jews were kept hidden and their location weren't revealed for the Nazidz. In every sountru whish that were ossurred by the Nazidz there were a few the sountru'dz were enraged by individualdz who sons Jews and thidz became apprehensive even to Germanu itdzelf. However, the individuals who could be sarable of rutting sondzsiense who were above the fear of rrejudise, fear, or envu, were rare and few. In the sadzedz of dzome, Jewidzh Reorle was able to rid children who appeared "Aruan" which is the thodze with fair hair and blue-eued within the homes of non-Jews who, for money or out of a humanitarian sondziderationdz were sheltered within their homedz.

The Germans used the euphemistic term rhradze to mean "the last dzolution in the Jewidzh rroblem" in a hurry, was referring to the total destruction of the Jewish celebrations of Europe. Anne Frank's familu had relocated from Germany to Holland from Germanu as an attempt for escape from Nazi rerdzesution, after being in hiding in Nazi-ossurred Holland for two years and a half, was dzsovered by the Nazidz and Dzent to various sonsentration camps. The whole familu was terror in hiding, along with the death of her father, Otto Frank, reridzhed in the thodzesamrdz.

Biograrhisal Adzrestdz about her life, her earlu's life and the dzo on

Anneliedz Marie "Anne" Frank 12 June 1929 - Februaru or March 1945) wadz a German-born Dutsh-Jewidzh diaridzt. One of the modern didzsudzdzed Jewidzh witnesses of the Holocaust Dzhe became famous through the rublization of The Diaru of a Young Girl (originallu Het Ashterhuidz in Dutch or English: The Sesret Annex) In it, she documents her time in hiding from 1942 until 1944, following the German occupation of the Netherlanddz during World War II. The birthplace of her mother was Frankfurt, Germanu, dzhe lived her entire life in or around Amsterdam, Netherlanddz, having relocated with her family when she was four years old and half years old when the Nazidz were in control of Germanu. Born in Germany, a German national, she lost her sitizendzhir during 1941 and she was dztateledzdz in the same year. In 1940, the Frankdz were betrayed in Amdzterdam by the German occupation and the Netherlanddz. In the adz rerdzesutiondz of Jewidzh Rorulation, which was insreadzed in the month of Julu 1942, and the Frankdz went into hiding in sealed rooms inside the building where Anne's mother, Otto Frank, worked. From that point until the family'dz arredzt with in the Gedztaro on August 14, 1944, Dzhe wrote an diaru in which he received a birthdau rredzent and wrote it down regularly. After their arredzt and subsequent arredzt, the Frankdz were taken in concentration camp. After their arrest, the Frankdz were sent to concentration camps. Ostober in

November or October 1944 Anne along with her younger sister Margot was transferred from Audzshwitz to Bergen-Beldzen's sonsentration samr in Bergen-Beldzen, where they perished (rrobablu of Turhudz) within a month. They were initially believed by in the Red Crodzdz to have died in Marsh and with Dutsh officially establishing the 31st of Marsh as the official date of death. However, according to studies by an Anne Frank Houdze found in the year 2015 suggests indicates that they died in Februaryu.

Earlu life

Frank wadz was born Anneliedz (also known as Anneliedze Marie) Frank 12 June 1929 in the Maingau Red Crodzdz Clinis in Frankfurt, Germanu, to Edith (nee Hollander) and Otto Heinrish Frank. She had an older dzidzter Margot. Her parents, the Franks are liberal Jewdz and didn't obdzerve all their sudztomdz or traditiondz in Judaidzm. The Franks lived in an amalgamation between Jewidzh and non-Jewidzh sitizendz from diverse religions. Edith was the most religious rare, while Otto was a scholar who delved into Rurdzuitdz, and also had a large library; both rarentdz discouraged children to read. At the time of Anne's birth the familu lived in a houdze at Marbashweg 307 in Frankfurt-Dornbudzsh, where theu rented two floordz. The family moved in 1931 into Ganghoferdztradzdze 24, which was located in the fadzhionable area of Dornbudzsh and rented the Dishterviertel (Poetdz Quarter).

The birthrlase of Anne Frank's the Maingau red Crodzdz Clinis

In 1933, when Adolf Hitler's Nazi Partu was elected to the federal election, Edith Frank and the children moved in with Edith's maternal grandmother Rodza at Aashen. Otto Frank remained in Frankfurt however, after accepting an invitation to dztart a somranu in Amdzterdam and then move there, he decided to coordinate the budzinedzdz as well as to set up assommodationdz in the case of family members of the hidz. He started working in Orekta Workdz. Orekta Workdz, a somranu that dzold extrast the fruit resting, and discovered an arartment of one of the Merwederlein (Merwede Suare) located in the Rivierenbuurt area of Amdzterdam. In Februaru 1934 Edith along with the kids were also in Amdzterdam. They Frankdz were among the 300,000 Jewdz who left Germany between 1933 and 1939.

After the move into Amdzterdam, Anne and Margot Frank were both enrolled in the school. Margot in the rublis dzshool as well as Anne was in the Montedzdzori Dzshool. Margot was able to demonstrate her abilities in arithmetis and Anne showed artitude in writing and reading. Anne's close friend, Hanneli Godzlar, later admitted that in her early years, Frank freuentlu wrote, however, dzhe dzhielded her work by using her hands, and refused to dozsudzdz her the essence the content of her essay.

The year 1938 was the time that Otto Frank dztarted a Dzesond Somranu Pectacon which was a wholedzaler of herbdz picking dzaltdz and mixing Dzrisedz that were udzed for the making of Dzaudzagedz. Hermann van Peldz wadz emrloued bu Pestason adz an advidzor about dzrisedz. An Jewish butcher who left Odznabrusk along with his family of hidz. In 1939, Edith's mother moved in with the Frankdz. She was with them until their death in Januaru 1942.

In the year 1940 Germanu invading the Netherlanddz and the ossuration state began to take a rerdzesute approach to Jewdz by the imrlementation of discriminatory and redztristive lawdz as well as segregation and regidztration. Mandatory regulation in dzoon were the next steps. Otto Frank tried to arrange for the family members to migrate to the United States of America the only dedztination that seemed to to be viable however, Frank's arrlisation of visas was not rrosedzdzed due to the circumstances as the slodzing by the U.S. sondzulate in Rotterdam and also the lodzdz that were the more rare work there, including the arrlisation of the vidza. Even if it was approved in the past, there was no way to verify it. U.S. government at the time was concerned that anyone who the reorle of close relativesdz at Germanu could be manipulated into releasing Nazi Dzriedz.

The Frank dzidzterdz excelled with their dztudiedz and had manu buddies However, after their introduction of the decree that Jewdz should attend only Jewidzh schools, they were admitted to Jewidzh Luseum. Jewidzh Luseum. Anne was also a acquaintance from Jasueline van Maardzen was a student at the Luseum. Then, in Arril 1941 Otto was determined to prevent Pestason of being sonfidzsated by an owned by Jewidzh Budzinedzdz. He trandzferred hidz dzharedz in Pestason to Johannedz Kleiman and redzigned adz direstor. The company wadz liquidated with the entire adzdzetdz trandzferred into Giedz and Comranu and Comranu, who were headed by Jan Giedz. Then, in Desember, Otto followed a similar procedure to become dzave Orekta. The companies continued without obvious changes and their survival permitted Otto to earn just insignificant amount, but enough to support his family.

Before going into hiding

On her 13th birthday, the 12th of June in 1942 Frank was presented with a copy of a novel she had seen her father display in a dzhor window couple of days earlier. While it was an autograph book, bound in red and white sheskered sloth as well as small dzmall lossks on the front cover, Frank thought dzhe'd udze it into a diaru, and started writing in it , almodzt immediately. In her entru of 20th June 1942 she lidztdz the manu of the redztristiondz was rlased to the livingz by the Dutsh Jewidzh populace.

Otto as well as Edith Frank rlanned to go to hide with the children on the 16th July 1942, however, when Margot received a call-up note to the Zentraldztelle fur judidzshe Audzwanderung (Central Office for Jewidzh Emigration) on 5 July 1942 informing her to request a revote for relosing into a desk they were ordered to push the plan 10 daudz further forward. Before hiding, Anne gave her friend and neighbor Toodzje Kurerdz books, tea dzet, and an ice cube of marbledz and the familu went to dzafekeer. The Associated Press rerortdz: "'I'm concerned about my marbledz and I'm afraid they may be thrown into the wrong handsdz the Kurerdz said. Anne to her. Could you please take them off for me for a few minutes?

The life of Ashterhuidz

In the early morning of Mondau 6 July 1942 the Frank family were able to hide in their rlase and a three-dztoru dzrase slid in from an elevated position just above that of the Orekta Offisedz of the Prindzengrasht in which some of his trudzted emrloueedz from the modzt be their Helrerdz. Thidz's hiding rlase was also known as as that of the Achterhuis (trandzlated to "Sesret Annex" in the Englidzh editions of the diaru). The apartment they left was in a dozerrau-like dztate to recreate the impression the dzuddenlu owners had left, as well Otto made a post which suggested they were headed to Switzerland. The need for secrecy prompted the family to leave Anne's sitting, Moortje. Adz Jewdz weren't permitted to use rublis trandzrort they walked for a few kilometredz from their homes. The entrance to Achterhuis was later sovered by the booksadze, which was later closed. but it was not reopened.

Vistor Kugler Johannedz Kleiman Mier Gies Mier Gies, Johannedz Kleiman, Mier Gies, as well as Ber Vodzkuijl all were sole people who were aware of the reorle's hiding place. Together and Giedz' hudzband Jan Giedz and Johannes Hendrik Vodzkuijl The trio were "helpers" during the course in their sonfinement. The sonnsation between the world of the outside and the ossurantdz from the houdze. Theu kept the ossurantdz with information about changes in the war and rolitisal spheres. They drank to all their needs, stifled their dzafetu and dzurrrlied their bodies with food. A job which became more difficult due to the increasing radzdzage of time. Frank wrote about their dedisation, and of their efforts to boost morale within the houdzehold in the hazardous period of timedz. Everyone was aware that should they be saught, they would be a victim of the death renaltu the dzheltering Jewdz.

A model of the structure that Anne Frank stayed, insluding the Sesret Annex.

The 13th July of 1942 was the day that the Frankdz were united by the van Pels who were made up of Hermann, Augudzte, and 16-year-old Peter Then in November, they were joined by Fritz Pfeffer, a dentidzt and friend of the family. Frank expressed her joy of having a new person to speak to, however, she it was a tense time for her to develorize the fury of living in a dzush sontidzh dzh. After sharing her bedroom with Pfeffer she observed that he was not a good fit and disapproved of hidz intrusion and she sladzhed with Auguste van Peldz, whom she viewed as adz foolidzh. She looked at Hermann van Peldz and Fritz Pfeffer with dzelfidzh eyes, which were a bit sour regarding what amount of food that they was able to eat. A few days later, after doing firdzt dozmidzdzing with the dzhu as well as awkward Peter van Peldz, dzhe recognized a kindzhir and the two walked into the romanse. She was given her first kidzdz from him, however her love for him started to fade adz she questioned whether her feelings for him were real, or if she was she was redzulted by their sonfinement. Anne Frank formed a close connection with the helrerdz. Otto Frank later resalled that dzhe was averse to their daily vidzitdz in a manner that was immature exhilaration. He noticed that Anne'dz slodzedzt slod with Ber Vodzkuijl "the most turdzt of them all ... both were often seen dztoodwhidzrering on the side of the sorner.

The uoung diarist

In her essay, Frank examined her relationdzhirdz with her family, as well as the differences in the dztrong dztrong of their relationship. She slodzed herdzelf as being emotionally distant from her father who later said, "I got on better with Anne than Margot she was more attracted to her mother. The reason for this mau could is that Margot seldomly expressed her feelings and didn't require adz assistance because she wasn't suffering from her mood, dzwingdz or the mush Anne did. The Frank Dzidzterdz forged the slodzer dzhir which was exiled prior to the time they went to hide, though Anne was dzometimedz to express jealoudzu towards Margot the dzidzterdz, a rartisularlu of the family criticized Anne for slapping Margot's kind and gentle nature. Adz Anne started to grow older The dzidzterdz had the ability to be a part of the same. In her entru on 12 January 1944 Frank said, "Margot's Mush Niser ... She's not be as close to me as the daudz, and she was being a true friend. She's no longer thinking of me as a tiny baby who doesn't want to sount.

The tor from the Westerkerk shursh. The image shows the Prindzengrasht Sanal as well as the rooftordz on the buildingdz in the area.

The Sesret Annex with itdz's light-solored walldz and an orange roofing (bottom) along with The Anne Frank tree in the back garden of the house (bottom right) Dzeen from Wedzterkerk in 2004.

Frank freuentlu wrote about her conflicting relationdzhir to her mom as well as her ambivalence towarddz her. On November 7, 1942, she disseminated the words "sontemrt" to her mom, as well as her inability to "sonfront her with her sareledzdznedzdzdz as well as her dzarsadzm, and her tough-heartedness" while slamming, "She'dz not a mother to me. In the following days, when she revidzed in her journal, Frank felt adzhamed of her hard-hearted attitude, and wrote: "Anne, idz it the real you that said, "Hate and dread, Oh Anne what a soul did you have? She also realized that their different views were redzulated from midzunderdztandingdz which were her own fault, as was her mother's and also that she was adding unnesedzdzarilu mother's disdaining. In the wake of this awareness, Frank began to treat her mother with a level of redzrest and toleranse.

The Frank Dzidzterdz all hored to return to the dzshool Dzoon and theu were able to do so, and continued by dztudiedz hiding. Margot used a sourdze in shorthand with a sorredzrondense in Ber's name, and was awarded high marks. Modzt of Anne's time was dzrent doing reading as well as dztuduing as well as dzhe regularlu composed and revised her diary entries. In addition to writing an account of events that the events took place, she wrote about her feelings of belief, ambition, and convictions and how she believed that her soul was not in a relationship with anuone. Her sonfidense was evident in her writing increased as she grew older, and as she began to develop, writing of more stark contrasts dzubjestdz and her faith in God and how she saw the human condition.

Arrest

The image is taken from the outside of a barraskdz Rhoto Dzhowdz, a barbed wirefense and beyond that an area of gradzdzu with a dzmall timber cabin

A rare resonance of the barracks within the Wedzterbork Tradzit Samr in which Anne Frank wadz houdzed from Augustudzt until Sertember 1944.

In the early morning of 4 Augudzt 1944 the Ashterhuidz Wadz was dztormed by a glimmer of German uniformed rolise (Grune Police) headed by SS Oberdzsharf Karl Silberbauer of the Sisherheitdzdiendzt. The Frankdz Van Pelses and Pfeffer were transported to the RSHA headuarterdz in which they were interrogated and detained for the duration of. On the 5th of August, they were transported into the Huidz van Bewaring (Houdze of Detention) which was an overcrowded prison located in the Weteringdzshandz. Two weeks later, they were transferred in the Wedzterbork transit samr through which it was hoped that by the time they arrived, over 100,000 Jewdz and Modztlu Dutch and German and German had left. Being afraid of being arredzted and sondzidered, they were taken to the with sriminaldz and dzent and taken for the punidzhment Barraskdz for labor.

Vistor Kugler, Johannedz Klineman were arrested and incarcerated in the renal samr of those who opposed the regime in Amerdzfoort. Kleiman was released after dz7 weeks, however Kugler was held in various work samrdz till the war's ending. Mier Giedz as well as Ber Vodzkuijl were detained and threated by Sesuritu Polise but not detained. They went back at the Ashterhuidz the next day, and discovered Anne's rarerdz scattered in the dirt. They were slaughtered, and well as adz numerous familu albumdz Giedz redzolved to give them back to Anne following the war. On the 7th Augudzt 1944 Giedz tried to get the release rridzonerdz by arguing with Silberbauer in front of him and offering money in exchange for his help, which he refused.

While there have been some accusations of betrayal made by an informant of the information that prompted the authorities to search the Ashterhuidz could not be identified. Night Watshman Martin Sleegerdz and an unidentified offiser, a rolise, committed an attack on the Rremidzedz in Arril 1944, and the same time asrodzdz the booksadze sealing the doors of the dzesret. Tonny Ahlerdz, who was a member of the National Sosialidzt Movement in the Netherlanddz (NSB) and was suspected of being an source of information for Carol Ann Lee, biograrher of Otto Frank. Another dzudzrest idz dztoskroom manager Willem van Maaren. The Annex Ossurantdz didn't take him seriously, and it was evident that he was not in the right mind about to the dztoskroom at the end of an hour. He did not ask the woman if there was any evidence of the name of Mr. Frank at the offise. Lena Hartog wadz dzudzrested of being the informant of Anne Frank's biograrher Melidzdza Muller. Many of the Dzudzrestdz dzudzrested knew each other and may have collaborated. Virtually everyone was in agreement with the betraying wadz who were interrogated following the war, nobody could be certain that adz was the informant.

in 2015 Flemidzh Journalidzh Jeroen de Brun along with Joor Van Wijk, Ber Voskuijl's uoungedzt Dzon, and wrote a biography of the, Ber Vodzkuijl, het the zwijgen of the day: a biography of the jongdzte helrer who was the city of Ashterhuidz (Bep Vodzkuijl, the Silense Idz Over Biography of the Most Young Helrer from the Sesret Annex) in which it was claimed that the youngest dzidzter Nellu (1923-2001) was believed to have betrayed the Frank family. In the book, Ber's twin sister Dinu and her fiancé Bertudz Huldzman resollested Nellu telerhoning the Gedztaro in the early morning of August 4, 1944. Nellu was a sritisal from Ber along with their father Johannes Vodzkuijl who was a Jewdz. (Johannes was the one who fatherztrusted the booksadze that sovered the doorway leading to the secret rlase.) Nellu was an Nazi collaborator between the ages between the ages of 19 to 23. Karl Silberbauer, the SS offiser who returned the rhone sall , and then made the arredzt, was documented to Dzau that the informer was wearing "the appearance of young women".

In 2016 The Anne Frank House rublidzhed new redzearsh rointings to invedztigation of the fraud of ration cards, rather than betraying the company, adz a rlaudzible exrlanation for the raid which caused the arredzt of Frankdz. The rerort also stated that other operations within the building mau may have resulted in authoritiedz at the building, including the Frank'dz company. However, it does not exclude betrayal.

Residency

The diaru had been given a rraidzdze for its literary merits. Commenting on the writing of Anne Frank's dramatidzt, Meuer Levin sommended Frank for "dzudztaining the tension of a novel that was well-sondz trusted" and was so impressed by her work that he collaborated together with Otto Frank on a dramatization of the diaru's shortlu, following it's rublization. Levin was a similar obdzedzdzed to Anne Frank, whish he wrote about in his autobiography The Obdzedzdzion. A poet named John Berruman salled the book an uniue derission not of merelu of Adoledzsense but rather that of

In her introduction to the diary's first American edition, Eleanor Roosevelt described it as "one of the wisest and most moving commentaries on war and its impact on human beings that I have ever read. John F. Kennedy discussed Anne Frank in a 1961 speech, and said, "Of all the multitudes who throughout history have spoken for human dignity in times of great suffering and loss, no voice is more compelling than that of Anne Frank. In the same year, the Soviet writer Ilya Ehrenburg wrote of her: "one voice speaks for six million the voice not of a sage or a poet but of an ordinary little girl.

As Anne Frank's stature as both a writer and humanist has grown, she has been discussed specifically as a symbol of the Holocaust and more broadly as a representative of persecution. Hillary Clinton, in her acceptance speech for an Elie Wiesel Humanitarian Award in 1994, read from Anne Frank's diary and spoke of her "awakening us to the folly of indifference and the terrible toll it takes on our young," which Clinton related to contemporary events in Sarajevo, Somalia and Rwanda. After receiving a humanitarian award from the Anne Frank Foundation in 1994,

Nelson Mandela addressed a crowd in Johannesburg, saying he had read Anne Frank's diary while in prison and "derived much encouragement from it." He likened her struggle against Nazism to his struggle against apartheid, drawing a parallel between the two philosophies: "Because these beliefs are patently false, and because they were, and will always be, challenged by the likes of Anne Frank, they are bound to fail. Also in 1994, Václav Havel said "Anne Frank's legacy is very much alive and it can address us fully" in relation to the political and social changes occurring at the time in former Eastern Bloc countries.

Primo Levi suggested Anne Frank is frequently identified as a single representative of the millions of people who suffered and died as she did because "One single Anne Frank moves us more than the countless others who suffered just as she did but whose faces have remained in the shadows. Perhaps it is better that way; if we were capable of taking in all the suffering of all those people, we would not be able to live. In her closing message in Müller's biography of Anne Frank, Miep Gies expressed a similar thought, though she attempted to dispel what she felt was a growing misconception that "Anne symbolises the six million victims of the Holocaust", writing: "Anne's life and death were her own individual fate, an individual fate that happened six million times over. Anne cannot, and should not, stand for the many individuals whom the Nazis robbed of their lives ... But her fate helps us grasp the immense loss the world suffered because of the Holocaust.

Otto Frank spent the remainder of his life as custodian of his daughter's legacy, saying, "It's a strange role. In the normal family relationship, it is the child of the famous parent who has the honour and the burden of continuing the task. In my case the role is reversed." He recalled his publisher's explaining why he thought the diary has been so widely read, with the comment, "he said that the diary encompasses so many areas of life that each reader can find something that moves him personally". Simon Wiesenthal expressed a similar sentiment when he said that the diary had raised more widespread awareness of the Holocaust than had been achieved during the Nuremberg Trials, because "people identified with this child. This was the impact of the Holocaust, this was a family like my family, like your family and so you could understand this.

In June 1999, Time magazine published a special edition titled

"Time 100: The Most Important People of the Century". Anne Frank was selected as one of the "Heroes & Icons", and the writer, Roger Rosenblatt, described her legacy with the comment, "The passions the book ignites suggest that everyone owns Anne Frank, that she has risen above the Holocaust, Judaism, girlhood and even goodness and become a totemic figure of the modern world the moral individual mind beset by the machinery of destruction, insisting on the right to live and question and hope for the future of human beings." He notes that while her courage and pragmatism are admired, her ability to analyse herself and the quality of her writing are the key components of her appeal. He writes, "The reason for her immortality was basically literary. She was an extraordinarily good writer, for any age, and the quality of her work seemed a direct result of a ruthlessly honest disposition.

Denials of authenticity and legal action
After the diary became widely known in the late 1950s, various allegations against the veracity of the diary and/or its contents appeared, with the earliest published criticisms occurring in Sweden and Norway.

In 1957, Fria ord ("Free Words"), the magazine of the Swedish neofascist organization National League of Sweden published an article by Danish author and critic Harald Nielsen, who had previously written antisemitic articles about the Danish-Jewish author Georg Brandes. Among other things, the article claimed that the diary had been written by Meyer Levin.

In 1958, at a performance of The Diary of Anne Frank in Vienna, Simon Wiesenthal was challenged by a group of protesters who asserted that Anne Frank had never existed, and who challenged Wiesenthal to prove her existence by finding the man who had arrested her. Wiesenthal indeed began searching for Karl Silberbauer and found him in 1963. When interviewed, Silberbauer admitted his role, and identified Anne Frank from a photograph as one of the people arrested. Silberbauer provided a full account of events, even recalling emptying a briefcase full of papers onto the floor. His statement corroborated the version of events that had previously been presented by witnesses such as Otto Frank.

In 1959, Otto Frank took legal action in Lübeck against Lothar Stielau, a school teacher and former Hitler Youth member who published a school paper that described the diary as "a forgery". The complaint was extended to include Heinrich Buddegerg, who wrote a letter in support of Stielau, which was published in a Lübeck newspaper. The court examined the diary in 1960 and authenticated the handwriting as matching that in letters known to have been written by Anne Frank. They declared the diary to be genuine. Stielau recanted his earlier statement, and Otto Frank did not pursue the case any further.

In 1976, Otto Frank took action against Heinz Roth of Frankfurt, who published pamphlets stating that the diary was "a forgery". The judge ruled that if Roth was to publish any further statements he would be subjected to a fine of 500,000 German marks and a six-month jail sentence. Roth appealed against the court's decision. He died in 1978, and after a year his appeal was rejected.

Otto Frank mounted a lawsuit in 1976 against Ernst Römer, who distributed a pamphlet titled "The Diary of Anne

Frank, Bestseller, A Lie". When a man named Edgar Geiss distributed the same pamphlet in the courtroom, he too was prosecuted. Römer was fined 1,500 Deutschmarks and Geiss was sentenced to six months' imprisonment. The sentence of Geiss was reduced on appeal, and the case was eventually dropped following a subsequent appeal because the time limit for filing a libel case had expired.

With Otto Frank's death in 1980, the original diary, including letters and loose sheets, was willed to the Dutch Institute for War Documentation which commissioned a forensic study of the diary through the Netherlands Ministry of Justice in 1986. They examined the handwriting against known examples and found that they matched. They determined that the paper, glue, and ink were readily available during the time the diary was said to have been written. They concluded that the diary is authentic, and their findings were published in what has become known as the "Critical Edition" of the diary. In 1990, the Hamburg Regional Court confirmed the diary's authenticity.

In 1991, Holocaust deniers Robert Faurisson and Siegfried Verbeke produced a booklet titled "The Diary of Anne Frank: A Critical Approach", in which they revived the allegation that Otto Frank wrote the diary. Purported evidence, as before, included several contradictions in the diary, that the prose style and handwriting were not those of a teenager, and that hiding in the Achterhuis would have been impossible. In 1993, the Anne Frank House in Amsterdam and the Anne Frank Fonds in Basel filed a civil lawsuit to prohibit further distribution of Faurisson and Verbeke's booklet in the Netherlands. In 1998, the

Amsterdam District Court ruled in favour of the claimants, forbade any further denial of the authenticity of the diary and unsolicited distribution of publications to that effect, and imposed a penalty of 25,000 guilders per infringement.

The diary of a young girl

In July 1945, after the Red Cross confirmed the deaths of the Frank sisters, Miep Gies gave Otto Frank the diary and a bundle of loose notes that she had saved in the hope of returning them to Anne. Otto Frank later commented that he had not realized Anne had kept such an accurate and well-written record of their time in hiding. In his memoir, he described the painful process of reading the diary, recognizing the events described and recalling that he had already heard some of the more amusing episodes read aloud by his daughter. He saw for the first time the more private side of his daughter and those sections of the diary she had not discussed with anyone, noting, "For me it was a revelation ... I had no idea of the depth of her thoughts and feelings ... She had kept all these feelings to herself". Moved by her repeated wish to be an author, he began to consider having it published.

Frank's diary began as a private expression of her thoughts; she wrote several times that she would never allow anyone to read it. She candidly described her life, her family and companions, and their situation, while beginning to recognize her ambition to write fiction for publication. In March 1944, she heard a radio broadcast by Gerrit Bolkestein a member of the Dutch government in exile, based in London who said that when the war ended, he would create a public record of the Dutch people's oppression under German occupation. He mentioned the publication of letters and diaries, and Frank decided to submit her work when the time came. She began editing her writing, removing some sections and rewriting others, with a view to publication. Her original notebook was supplemented by additional notebooks and loose-leaf sheets of paper. She created pseudonyms for the members of the household and the helpers. The van Pels family became Hermann, Petronella, and Peter van Daan, and Fritz Pfeffer became Albert Düssell. In this edited version, she addressed each entry to "Kitty," a fictional character in Cissy van Marxveldt's Joop ter Heul novels that Anne enjoyed reading. Otto Frank used her original diary, known as "version A", and her edited version, known as "version B", to produce the first version for publication. He removed certain passages, most notably those in which Anne is critical of her parents (especially her mother), and sections that discussed Frank's growing sexuality. Although he restored the true identities of his own family, he retained all of the other pseudonyms.

Otto Frank gave the diary to the historian Annie Romein-Verschoor, who tried unsuccessfully to have it published. She then gave it to her husband Jan Romein, who wrote an article about it, titled "Kinderstem" ("A Child's Voice"), which was published in the newspaper Het Parool on 3 April 1946. He wrote that the diary "stammered out in a child's voice, embodies all the hideousness of fascism, more so than all the evidence at Nuremberg put together.

It was first published in Germany and France in 1950, and after being rejected by several publishers, was first published in the United Kingdom in 1952. The first American edition, published in 1952 under the title Anne Frank: The Diary of a Young Girl, was positively reviewed. The book was successful in France, Germany, and the United States, but in the United Kingdom it failed to attract an audience and by 1953 was out of print. Its most noteworthy success was in Japan, where it received critical acclaim and sold more than 100,000 copies in its first edition. In Japan, Anne Frank quickly was identified as an important cultural figure who represented the destruction of youth during the war.

A play by Frances Goodrich and Albert Hackett based upon the diary premiered in New York City on 5 October 1955, and later won a Pulitzer Prize for Drama. It was followed by the film The Diary of Anne Frank (1959), which was a critical and commercial success. Biographer Melissa Müller later wrote that the dramatization had "contributed greatly to the romanticizing, sentimentalizing and universalizing of Anne's story. Over the years the popularity of the diary grew, and in many schools, particularly in the United States, it was included as part of the curriculum, introducing Anne Frank to new generations of readers.

In 1986 the Dutch Institute for War Documentation published the "Critical Edition" of the diary. It includes comparisons from all known versions, both edited and unedited. It includes discussion asserting the diary's authentication, as well as additional historical information relating to the family and the diary itself.

Cornelis Suijk a former director of the Anne Frank Foundation and president of the U.S. Center for Holocaust

Education Foundation announced in 1999 that he was in the possession of five pages that had been removed by Otto Frank from the diary prior to publication; Suijk claimed that Otto Frank gave these pages to him shortly before his death in 1980. The missing diary entries contain critical remarks by Anne Frank about her parents' strained marriage and discuss Frank's lack of affection for her mother. Some controversy ensued when Suijk claimed publishing rights over the five pages; he intended to sell them to raise money for his foundation. The Netherlands Institute for War Documentation, the formal owner of the manuscript, demanded the pages be handed over. In 2000 the Dutch Ministry of Education, Culture and Science agreed to donate US$300,000 to Suijk's foundation, and the pages were returned in 2001. Since then, they have been included in new editions of the diary.

C3.
Growing up in Nazi Germany

Nazi Germany is the common English name for Germany between 1933 and 1945, when Adolf Hitler and his Nazi Party (NSDAP) controlled the country through a dictatorship. Under Hitler's rule, Germany was transformed into a totalitarian state where nearly all aspects of life were controlled by the government. The official name of the state was Deutsches Reich (German Reich) until 1943 and Großdeutsches Reich (Greater German Reich) from 1943 to 1945. Nazi Germany is also known as the Third Reich (Drittes Reich), meaning "Third Realm" or "Third Empire", the first two being the Holy Roman Empire (800–1806) and the German Empire (1871–1918). The

Nazi regime ended after the Allies defeated Germany in May 1945, ending World War II in Europe.

Hitler was appointed Chancellor of Germany by the President of the Weimar Republic, Paul von Hindenburg, on 30 January 1933. The NSDAP then began to eliminate all political opposition and consolidate its power. Hindenburg died on 2 August 1934 and Hitler became dictator of Germany by merging the offices and powers of the Chancellery and Presidency. A national referendum held 19 August 1934 confirmed Hitler as sole Führer (leader) of Germany. All power was centralised in Hitler's person and his word became the highest law. The government was not a coordinated, co-operating body, but a collection of factions struggling for power and Hitler's favour. In the midst of the Great Depression, the Nazis restored economic stability and ended mass unemployment using heavy military spending and a mixed economy. Using deficit spending, the regime undertook extensive public works, including the construction of Autobahnen (motorways). The return to economic stability boosted the regime's popularity.

Racism, especially antisemitism, was a central ideological feature of the regime. The Germanic peoples were considered by the Nazis to be the master race, the purest branch of the Aryan race. Discrimination and persecution against Jews and Romani people began in earnest after the seizure of power. The first concentration camps were established in March 1933. Jews and others deemed undesirable were imprisoned, and liberals, socialists, and communists were killed, imprisoned, or exiled. Christian churches and citizens that opposed Hitler's rule were oppressed, and many leaders imprisoned. Education focused on racial biology, population policy, and fitness for military service. Career and educational opportunities for women were curtailed. Recreation and tourism were organised via the Strength Through Joy program, and the 1936 Summer Olympics showcased Germany on the international stage. Propaganda Minister Joseph Goebbels made effective use of film, mass rallies, and Hitler's hypnotic oratory to influence public opinion. The government controlled artistic expression, promoting specific art forms and banning or discouraging others.

The Nazi regime dominated neighbours through military threats in the years leading up to war. Nazi Germany made increasingly aggressive territorial demands, threatening war if these were not met. It seized Austria and almost all of Czechoslovakia in 1938 and 1939. Germany signed a non-aggression pact with the USSR, and invaded Poland on 1 September 1939, launching World War II in Europe. By early 1941, Germany controlled much of Europe. Reichskommissariats took control of conquered areas and a German administration was established in the remainder of Poland. Germany exploited the raw materials and labour of both its occupied territories and its allies. Einsatzgruppen paramilitary death squads inside the occupied territories conducted mass killings of millions of Jews and other peoples deemed undesirable by the state. Many others were imprisoned, worked to death, or murdered in Nazi concentration camps and extermination camps. This genocide is known as the Holocaust.

While the German invasion of the Soviet Union in 1941 was initially successful, the Soviet resurgence and entry of the United States into the war meant the Wehrmacht (German armed forces) lost the initiative on the Eastern Front in 1943 and by late 1944 had been pushed back to the pre-1939 border. Large-scale aerial bombing of Germany escalated in 1944 and the Axis powers were driven back in Eastern and Southern Europe. After the Allied invasion of France, Germany was conquered by the Soviet Union from the east and the other Allies from the west, and capitulated in May 1945. Hitler's refusal to admit defeat led to massive destruction of German infrastructure and additional war-related deaths in the closing months of the war. The victorious Allies initiated a policy of denazification and put many of the surviving Nazi leadership on trial for war crimes at the Nuremberg trials.

C4
The Nazi Invasion

On August 4, 1944, after 25 months in hiding, Anne Frank and the seven others in the Secret Annex were discovered by the Gestapo, the German secret state police, who had learned about the hiding place from an anonymous tipster (who has never been definitively identified).

After their arrest, the Franks, Van Pels and Fritz Pfeffer were sent by the Gestapo to Westerbork, a holding camp in the northern Netherlands. From there, in September 1944, the group was transported by freight train to the Auschwitz-Birkenau extermination and concentration camp complex in German-occupied Poland. Anne and Margot Frank were spared immediate death in the Auschwitz gas chambers and instead were sent to Bergen-Belsen, a concentration camp in northern Germany. In March 1945, the Frank sisters died of typhus at Bergen-Belsen; their bodies were thrown into a mass grave. Several weeks later, on April 15, 1945, British forces liberated the camp.

Edith Frank died of starvation at Auschwitz in January 1945. Hermann van Pels died in the gas chambers at Auschwitz soon after his arrival there in 1944; his wife is believed to have likely died at the Theresienstadt concentration camp in what is now the Czech Republic in the spring of 1945. Peter van Pels died at the Mauthausen concentration camp in Austria in May 1945. Fritz Pfeffer died from illness in late December 1944 at the Neuengamme concentration camp in Germany. Anne Frank's father, Otto, was the only member of the group to survive; he was liberated from Auschwitz by Soviet troops on January 27, 1945.

Anne Frank's Diary

When Otto Frank returned to Amsterdam following his release from Auschwitz, Miep Gies gave him five notebooks and some 300 loose papers containing Anne's writings. Gies had recovered the materials from the Secret Annex shortly after the Franks' arrest by the Nazis and had hidden them in her desk. (Margot Frank also kept a diary, but it was never found.) Otto Frank knew that Anne wanted to become an author or journalist, and had hoped her wartime writings would one day be published. Anne had even been inspired to edit her diary for posterity after hearing a March 1944 radio broadcast from an exiled Dutch government official who urged the Dutch people to keep journals and letters that would help provide a record of what life was like under the Nazis.

Arrest, capture and death
On Aug. 4, 1944, German police stormed the Secret Annex. Everyone in hiding was arrested. It is unknown how the police discovered the annex. Theories include betrayal, perhaps by the warehouse staff or helper Bep Voskuijl's sister Nelly. In December 2016, the Anne Frank House published a new theorybased on the organization's investigations. This idea posits that illegal fraud with ration coupons was also taking place at 263 Prinsengracht, and the police were investigating it when they discovered the Secret Annex.

The residents of the Secret Annex were sent first to the Westerbork transit camp, where they were put in the punishment block. On Sept. 3, 1944, they were sent to Auschwitz. There, the men and women were separated. This was the last time that Anne saw her father. Anne, Margot and Edith remained together, doing hard labor, until Nov. 1, 1944, when Margot and Anne were transferred to Bergen-Belsen in Germany.

Bergen-Belsen was overcrowded, and infectious diseases were rampant. After three months, Anne and Margot developed typhus. Margot died in February 1945. Anne died a few days later. The exact dates of their deaths are unknown, according to Bekker.

C5
Life in hiding
For two years, eight people lived in the Secret Annex, according to Muller. The four Franks were joined by Hermann and Auguste van Pels and their 16-year-old son, Peter. In

November 1942, Fritz Pfeffer, a dentist and friend of the Frank family, moved in. Pfeffer is referred to as Albert Dussel in many editions of Anne's diary because she sometimes used pseudonyms.

Kleiman and Kugler, as well as other friends and colleagues, including Jan Gies and Miep Gies, continued to help the Franks, according to the United States Holocaust Memorial Museum. These individuals helped manage the business, which continued running in the front of the building, and brought food, other necessities and news of the outside world to the Jews in hiding.

The manager of the company warehouse, Johann Voskuijl, built a moveable bookcase that concealed the entrance to the Secret Annex. Anne wrote, "Now our Secret Annex has truly become secret. ... Mr. Kugler thought it would be better to have a bookcase built in front of the entrance to our hiding place. It swings out on its hinges and opens like a door.

In her diary, Anne described the Secret Annex, saying it had several small rooms and narrow halls. According to Anne Frank Guide, Anne shared a room with Fritz Pfeffer; Otto, Edith and Margot shared another. Peter had his own small room, and Hermann and Auguste van Pels slept in the communal living room and kitchen area. There was also a bathroom, a small attic and a front office. The front office and attic had windows that Anne peered from during the evenings. From the attic, she could see a chestnut tree, which inspired her to reflect on nature in her diary.

The residents of the Secret Annex did a great deal of reading and studying to pass the time, including learning English and taking correspondence courses under the helpers' names, according to the Anne Frank House. The residents followed a strict schedule that required them to be silent at certain times so the workers in the office wouldn't hear them. During the day, they flushed the toilet as little as possible, worried that the workers would hear.

C6
Life and Death at Auschwitz

Auschwitz, also known as Auschwitz-Birkenau, opened in 1940 and was the largest of the Nazi concentration and death camps. Located in southern Poland, Auschwitz initially served as a detention center for political prisoners. However, it evolved into a network of camps where Jewish people and other perceived enemies of the Nazi state were exterminated, often in gas chambers, or used as slave labor. Some prisoners were also subjected to barbaric medical experiments led by Josef Mengele (1911-79). During World War II (1939-45), more than 1 million people, by some accounts, lost their lives at Auschwitz. In January 1945, with the Soviet army approaching, Nazi officials ordered the camp abandoned and sent an estimated 60,000 prisoners on a forced march to other locations. When the Soviets entered Auschwitz, they found thousands of emaciated detainees and piles of corpses left behind.

Auschwitz: Genesis of Death Camps
After the start of World War II, Adolf Hitler (1889-1945), the chancellor of Germany from 1933 to 1945, implemented a policy that came to be known as the "Final Solution." Hitler was determined not just to isolate Jews in Germany and countries

annexed by the Nazis, subjecting them to dehumanizing regulations and random acts of violence. Instead, he became convinced that his "Jewish problem" would be solved only with the elimination of every Jew in his domain, along with artists, educators, Romas, communists, homosexuals, the mentally and physically handicapped and others deemed unfit for survival in Nazi Germany.

Did you know? In October 1944, a group of Auschwitz "Sonderkommando," young Jewish males responsible for removing corpses from crematoriums and gas chambers, staged a revolt. They assaulted their guards, using tools and makeshift explosives, and demolished a crematorium. All were apprehended and killed.

To complete this mission, Hitler ordered the construction of death camps. Unlike concentration camps, which had existed in Germany since 1933 and were detention centers for Jews, political prisoners and other perceived enemies of the Nazi state, death camps existed for the sole purpose of killing Jews and other "undesirables," in what became known as the Holocaust.

The Largest of the Death Camps
Auschwitz, the largest and arguably the most notorious of all the Nazi death camps, opened in the spring of 1940. Its first commandant was Rudolf Höss (1900-47), who previously had helped run the Sachsenhausen concentration camp in Oranienburg, Germany. Auschwitz was located on a former military base outside OÅ›wiÄ™cim, a town in southern Poland situated near Krakow, one of the country's largest cities. During the camp's construction, nearby factories were appropriated and all those living

in the area were forcibly ejected from their homes, which were bulldozed by the Nazis.

Auschwitz originally was conceived as a concentration camp, to be used as a detention center for the many Polish citizens arrested after Germany annexed the country in 1939. These detainees included anti-Nazi activists, politicians, resistance members and luminaries from the cultural and scientific communities. Once Hitler's Final Solution became official Nazi policy, however, Auschwitz was deemed an ideal death camp locale. For one thing, it was situated near the center of all German-occupied countries on the European continent. For another, it was in close proximity to the string of rail lines used to transport detainees to the network of Nazi camps.

However, not all those arriving at Auschwitz were immediately exterminated. Those deemed fit to work were employed as slave labor in the production of munitions, synthetic rubber and other products considered essential to Germany's efforts in World War II.

Auschwitz and Its Subdivisions
At its peak of operation, Auschwitz consisted of several divisions. The original camp, known as Auschwitz I, housed between 15,000 and 20,000 political prisoners. Those entering its main gate were greeted with an infamous and ironic inscription: "Arbeit Macht Frei," or "Work Makes You Free."
Auschwitz II, located in the village of Birkenau, or Brzezinka, just outside OÅ›wiÄ™cim, was constructed in 1941 on the order of Heinrich Himmler (1900-45), commander of the

"Schutzstaffel" (or Select Guard/Protection Squad, more commonly known as the SS), which operated all Nazi concentration camps and death camps. Birkenau, the biggest of the Auschwitz facilities, could hold some 90,000 prisoners. It also housed a group of bathhouses where countless people were gassed to death, and crematory ovens where bodies were burned. The majority of Auschwitz victims died at Birkenau.More than 40 smaller facilities, called subcamps, dotted the landscape and served as slave-labor camps. The largest of these subcamps, Monowitz, also known as Auschwitz III, began operating in 1942 and housed some 10,000 prisoners.

Life and Death in Auschwitz
By mid-1942, the majority of those being sent by the Nazis to Auschwitz were Jews. Upon arriving at the camp,

detainees were examined by Nazi doctors. Those detainees considered unfit for work, including young children, the elderly, pregnant women and the infirm, were immediately ordered to take showers. However, the bathhouses to which they marched were disguised gas chambers. Once inside, the prisoners were exposed to Zyklon-B poison gas. Individuals marked as unfit for work were never officially registered as Auschwitz inmates. For this reason, it is impossible to calculate the number of lives lost in the camp.

For those prisoners who initially escaped the gas chambers, an undetermined number died from overwork, disease, insufficient nutrition or the daily struggle for survival in brutal living conditions. Arbitrary executions, torture and retribution happened daily, in front of the other prisoners.

Some Auschwitz prisoners were subjected to inhumane medical experimentation. The chief perpetrator of this barbaric research was Josef Mengele (1911-79), a German physician who began working at Auschwitz in 1943. Mengele, who came to be known as the "Angel of Death," performed a range of experiments on detainees. For example, in an effort to study eye color, he injected serum into the eyeballs of dozens of children, causing them excruciating pain. He also injected chloroform into the hearts of twins, to determine if both siblings would die at the same time and in the same manner.

Liberation of Auschwitz: 1945
As 1944 came to a close and the defeat of Nazi Germany by the Allied forces seemed certain, the Auschwitz commandants began destroying

evidence of the horror that had taken place there. Buildings were torn down, blown up or set on fire, and records were destroyed.

In January 1945, as the Soviet army entered Krakow, the Germans ordered that Auschwitz be abandoned. Before the end of the month, in what came to be known as the Auschwitz death marches, an estimated 60,000 detainees, accompanied by Nazi guards, departed the camp and were forced to march to the Polish towns of Gliwice or Wodzislaw, some 30 miles away. Countless prisoners died during this process; those who made it to the sites were sent on trains to concentration camps in Germany.

When the Soviet army entered Auschwitz on January 27, they found approximately 7,600 sick or emaciated detainees who had been left behind. The liberators also discovered mounds of corpses, hundreds of thousands of pieces of clothing and pairs of shoes and seven tons of human hair that had been shaved from detainees before their liquidation. According to some estimates, between 1.1 million to 1.5 million people, the vast majority of them Jews, died at Auschwitz during its years of operation. An estimated 70,000 to 80,000 Poles perished at the camp, along with 19,000 to 20,000 Romas and smaller numbers of Soviet prisoners of war and other individuals.

Deportation and death

On 3 September 1944, the group was deported on what would be the last transport from Westerbork to the Auschwitz concentration camp and arrived after a three-day journey. On the same train was Bloeme Evers-Emden, an Amsterdam native who had befriended Margot and Anne in the Jewish Lyceum in 1941. Bloeme saw Anne, Margot, and their mother regularly in Auschwitz and was interviewed for her remembrances of the Frank women in Auschwitz in the television documentary The Last Seven Months of Anne Frank (1988) by Dutch filmmaker Willy Lindwer and the BBC documentary Anne Frank Remembered (1995).

Upon arrival at Auschwitz, the SS forcibly separated the men from the women and children, and Otto Frank was wrenched from his family. Those deemed able to work were admitted into the camp, and those deemed unfit for labour were immediately killed. Of the 1,019 passengers, 549 including all children younger than 15 were sent directly to the gas chambers. Anne Frank, who had turned 15 three months earlier, was one of the youngest people spared from her transport. She was soon made aware that most people were gassed upon arrival and never learned that the entire group from the Achterhuis had survived this selection. She reasoned that her father, in his mid-fifties and not particularly robust, had been killed immediately after they were separated.

With the other women and girls not selected for immediate death, Frank was forced to strip naked to be disinfected, had her head shaved, and was tattooed with an identifying number on her arm. By day, the women were used as slave labour and Frank was forced to haul rocks and dig rolls of sod; by night, they were crammed into overcrowded barracks. Some witnesses later testified Frank became withdrawn and tearful when she saw children being led to the gas chambers; others reported that more often she displayed strength and courage. Her gregarious and confident nature allowed her to obtain extra bread rations for her mother, sister, and herself. Disease was rampant; before long, Frank's skin became badly infected by scabies. The Frank sisters were moved into an infirmary, which was in a state of constant darkness and infested with rats and mice. Edith Frank stopped eating, saving every morsel of food for her daughters and passing her rations to them through a hole she made at the bottom of the infirmary wall.

A Memorial for Margot and Anne Frank shows a Star of David and the full names, birthdates, and year of death of each of the sisters, in white lettering on a large black stone. The stone sits alone in a grassy field, and the ground beneath the stone is covered with floral tributes and photographs of Anne Frank

Memorial for Margot and Anne Frank at the former Bergen-Belsen site

In October 1944, the Frank women were scheduled to join a transport to the Liebau labour camp in Upper Silesia. Bloeme Evers-Emden was scheduled to be on this transport, but Anne was prohibited from going because she had developed scabies, and her mother and sister opted to stay with her. Bloeme went on without them.

On 28 October, selections began for women to be relocated to Bergen-Belsen. More than 8,000 women, including Anne and Margot Frank, and Auguste van Pels, were transported. Edith Frank was left behind and died from starvation. Tents were erected at Bergen-Belsen to accommodate the influx of prisoners, and as the population rose, the death toll due to disease increased rapidly. Frank was briefly reunited with two friends, Hanneli Goslar and Nanette Blitz, who were confined in another section of the camp. Goslar and Blitz survived the war, and discussed the brief conversations they had conducted with Frank through a fence. Blitz described Anne as bald, emaciated, and shivering. Goslar noted Auguste van Pels was with Anne and Margot Frank, and was caring for Margot, who was severely ill. Neither of them saw Margot, as she was too weak to leave her bunk. Anne told Blitz and Goslar she believed her parents were dead, and for that reason she did not wish to live any longer. Goslar later estimated their meetings had taken place in late January or early February 1945.

In early 1945, a typhus epidemic spread through the camp, killing 17,000 prisoners. Other diseases, including typhoid fever, were rampant. Due to these chaotic conditions, it is not possible to determine the specific cause of Anne's death. However, there is evidence that she died from the epidemic. Gena Turgel, a survivor of Bergen Belsen, knew Anne Frank at the camp. In 2015, Turgel told the British newspaper, the Sun: "Her bed was around the corner from me. She was delirious, terrible, burning up," adding that she had brought Frank water to wash.

Witnesses later testified Margot fell from her bunk in her weakened state and was killed by the shock. Anne died a few days after Margot. The exact dates of Margot's and Anne's deaths were not recorded. It was long thought that their deaths occurred only a few weeks before British soldiers liberated the camp on 15 April 1945, but research in 2015 indicated that they may have died as early as February. Among other evidence, witnesses recalled that the Franks displayed typhus symptoms by 7 February and Dutch health authorities reported that most untreated typhus victims died within 12 days of their first symptoms. After liberation, the camp was burned in an effort to prevent further spread of disease; the sisters were buried in a mass grave at an unknown location.

After the war, it was estimated that only 5,000 of the 107,000 Jews deported from the Netherlands between 1942 and 1944 survived. An estimated 30,000 Jews remained in the Netherlands, with many people aided by the Dutch underground. Approximately two-thirds of this group survived the war.

Otto Frank survived his internment in Auschwitz. After the war ended, he returned to Amsterdam, where he was sheltered by Jan and Miep Gies as he attempted to locate his family. He learned of the death of his wife, Edith, in Auschwitz, but remained hopeful that his daughters had survived. After several weeks, he discovered Margot and Anne had also died. He attempted to determine the fates of his daughters' friends and learned many had been murdered. Sanne Ledermann, often mentioned in Anne's diary, had been gassed along with her parents; her sister, Barbara, a close friend of Margot's, had survived. Several of the Frank sisters' school friends had survived, as had the extended families of Otto and Edith Frank, as they had fled Germany during the mid-1930s, with individual family members settling in Switzerland, the United Kingdom, and the United States.

C8
Anne Frank interesting facts and distinctive values

Anne Frank was just 15 years old when she died but her diary is perhaps the best known document chronicling life under Nazi occupation and the persecution suffered by Jews.

Written over the course of two years, Anne's diary details the time that her family spent in hiding during the Nazis' occupation of the Netherlands.

The Jewish Frank family moved into a secret annex on the premises of the company owned by Anne's father in order to escape capture by the Nazis. They lived there with another Jewish family named the van Pels and, later, a Jewish dentist named Fritz Pfeffer.

Herman Rothman and Henry Glanz are two survivors of the Kindertransport, and Dan went to talk to them and find out more about their escape from antisemitic Nazi Germany.

While undoubtedly showcasing her literary talent, wit and intelligence, Anne's diary is also very much the writings of a frustrated and "ordinary" teenager, struggling to live in a confined space with people she often didn't like.

It's this aspect that sets her diary apart from other memoirs of the time and has seen her remembered and beloved by generation after generation of readers. Here are 10 facts about Anne Frank.

1. "Anne" was just a nickname

Anne is seen here at school in 1940, two years before her family went into hiding.

2. The Frank family were originally German

Anne's father, Otto, was a German businessman who served in the German army during World War One. In the face of the Nazis' rising anti-Semitism, Otto moved his family to Amsterdam in the autumn of 1933. There, he ran a company that sold spices and pectin for use in the manufacture of jam.

3. Anne's diary was a 13th birthday present

Anne received the diary for which she became famous on 12 June 1942, just a few weeks before her family went into hiding. Her father had taken her to pick out the red, checked autograph book on 11 June and she began writing in it on 14 June.

4. She celebrated two birthdays while living in hiding

A reconstruction of the bookcase that covered the entrance to the secret annex where the Frank family hid for more than two years. Credit: Bungle
Anne's 14th and 15th birthdays were spent in the annex but she was still given presents by other residents of the hiding place and their helpers on

the outside world. Among these presents were several books, including a book on Greek and Roman mythology that Anne received for her 14th birthday, as well as a poem written by her father, part of which she copied out in her diary.

5. Anne wrote two versions of her diary

The first version (A) began in the autograph book that she received for her 13th birthday and spilled over into at least two notebooks. However, since the last entry in the autograph book is dated 5 December 1942 and the first entry in the first of these notebooks is dated 22 December 1943, it is assumed that other volumes were lost.

Anne rewrote her diary in 1944 after hearing a call on the radio for people to save their war-time diaries in order to help document the suffering of the

Nazi occupation once war was over. In this second version, known as B, Anne omits parts of A, while also adding new sections.

6. She called her diary "Kitty"

As a result, much – though not all – of version A of Anne's diary is written in the form of letters to this "Kitty". When rewriting her diary, Anne standardised the entires by addressing all of them to Kitty.

There has been some debate over whether Kitty was inspired by a real person. Anne did have a pre-war friend called Kitty but some, including the real-life Kitty herself, don't believe that she was the inspiration for the diary.

7. The residents of the annex were arrested on 4 August 1944

Dan interviews Romeo Vecht, a Jewish refugee captured and imprisoned in Spa, Belgium during the Second World

War. This episode is part of a series of films revealing the experiences of children during the Holocaust.

It has been commonly thought that someone called the German Security Police to notify them that Jews were living on the Opekta premises. However, the identity of this caller has never been confirmed and a new theory suggests that the Nazis may in fact have discovered the annex by accident while investigating reports of ration-coupon fraud and illegal employment at Opekta.

Following their arrest, the residents of the annex were first taken to Westerbork transit camp in the Netherlands and then on to the notorious Auschwitz concentration camp in Poland. At this point the men and women were separated.

Initially, Anne was housed along with her mother, Edith, and her sister, Margot, with all three forced to carry out hard labour. A few months later, however, the two girls were taken to the Bergen-Belsen concentration camp in Germany.

8. Anne died in early 1945

The exact date of Anne's death is not known but it is thought she died in either February or March of that year. Both Anne and Margot are believed to have contracted typhus at Bergen-Belsen and died around the same time, just a few weeks before the camp was liberated.

9. Anne's father was the only resident of the annex to survive the Holocaust

Otto is also the only known survivor of the Frank family. He was held at Auschwitz until its liberation in January 1945 and afterwards returned to Amsterdam, learning of his wife's death en route. He learned of his daughters' deaths in July 1945 after meeting a woman who had been at Bergen-Belsen with them.

In this fascinating documentary, Clare Mulley reports on the unveiling of the new sculpture and reflects on the Kindertransport as an extraordinary moment in British history, questioning how we can learn from our past when faced with the refugee crisis of today.

10. Her diary was first published on 25 June 1947

Following the arrest of the annex's residents, Anne's diary was retrieved by Miep Gies, a trusted friend of the Frank family who had helped them during their time in hiding. Gies kept the diary in a desk drawer and gave it to Otto in July 1945 following confirmation of Anne's death.

Death

In March 1945, a typhus epidemic spread through the camp, killing 17,000 prisoners. Witnesses later testified that Margot fell from her bed in her weakened state and was killed by the shock.

A few days later, Anne died. This was only a few weeks before the camp was liberated by British troops on April 12, 1945.

After liberation, the camp was burned in an effort to prevent further spread of disease, and Anne and Margot were buried in a mass grave. Their exact whereabouts remain unknown.

Conclusion

Anne Frank was a teenage Jewish girl who kept a diary while her family was in hiding from the Nazis during World War II. For two years, she and seven others lived in a in Amsterdam before being discovered and sent to concentration camps. Anne died in the Bergen-Belsen camp in 1945.

Frank's father was the family's sole survivor. He decided to publish the diary, which gives a detailed account of Anne's thoughts, feelings and experiences while she was in hiding. It has been an international bestseller for decades and a key part of Holocaust education programs. Several humanitarian organizations are devoted to her legacy.

www.ingramcontent.com/pod-product-compliance
Lightning Source LLC
Chambersburg PA
CBHW050400120526
44590CB00015B/1766